One Year to a College Degree

by Lynette Long
and
Eileen Hershberger

HUNTINGTON HOUSE PUBLISHERS

Huntington House Publishers
P.O. Box 53788
Lafayette, Louisiana 70505

Library of Congress Card Catalog Number 91-72905
ISBN 1-56384-001-4

CONTENTS

CHAPTER 1
LIVING PROOF

The year is 1962. John F. Kennedy is president. *Lawrence of Arabia* is the Best Picture of the Year. John Glen orbits the earth. Marilyn Monroe dies of a drug overdose. I flunk out of my freshman year in a liberal arts junior college. I hear my mother telling me, "You don't study hard enough." I get a job as a clerk-typist using an old Royal manual typewriter.

For me, the year 1962 was both good and bad. I left school for a job in what I saw as the real world. I started getting a regular salary and went right out and bought my first car. I was no longer a schoolgirl; I was a working woman.

After twenty-eight years of moving around Washington, DC, from the State Department to the White House, then to the Treasury Department and, finally, to the Department of Agriculture, my career growth eventually stopped. Here I was, a mid-level management analyst, stuck on the middle rung of my career ladder without a college degree, but sitting on top of a pile of certificates and performance commendations testifying that I had successfully completed over a dozen administrative, managerial, computer, and business-related courses and jobs. Without a college degree, I seemed to be forever stuck at mid-level.

Every year at least once, usually around New Year's resolution time, I would entertain the idea of somehow going back to college to get a degree. Every year, though, I made excuses and came up with logical reasons to convince myself the effort of returning to school wasn't worth it. My excuses included needing to spend what free time I had with my two daughters, being too depressed following young widowhood to concentrate on academics, anxiety about not being able to do school work after being out of school for so long, my fear of being in classes with kids who were twenty years younger, to the fact that college on a part-time basis would probably take seven or eight years to get a degree.

I came close to going back to school in 1980 when I enrolled in the American University's APEL Program (Assessment of Prior Experiential Learning). I earned twenty-six credits for describing the knowledge I got from doing ordinary things like working for the government, landscaping my yard, taking photos of kids at my daughters' schools and camps and selling them to parents, and coaching a girls' basketball team. When I realized that even after getting these twenty-six credits I was still years away from a degree, I lost heart and dropped the idea again.

Having only 14 credits from junior college, which would be accepted at another school as transfer credits, and 26 credits from American University, I still needed 80 more credits to total the 120 credits required for a degree. If I took two classes a semester and registered every semester, I could earn twelve credits a year. At that rate it would take me seven years to get a degree. All I could think of was seven long, hard, little free time, no socializing, no-time-for-anything-else years.

In January 1990, Dr. Long, a recent professor at American University, urged me to enroll at Maryland University for the spring semester, which was due to start the following week. Thinking that the many work-related courses and seminars for which I had certificates would be creditable toward a degree, she said I would have a good chance of earning my degree in less than two years. Since two years was just a fraction of my earlier time projection, and because it voided my usual argument that college would take too long, I agreed to talk to someone in the adult education department about registering.

Dr. Long, understanding my fears, literally led me by the hand to the Adult Education Center at the University of Maryland and through the maze of signs all over the place directing students, THIS WAY FOR RE-REGISTRATION,

LINE UP HERE FOR GRADUATE COURSES, HERE FOR NEW STUDENT APPLICATIONS. I had no idea a university was this complicated. My mother had taken complete charge of deciding on and registering me for junior college. I didn't have to do a thing or stand in any line. I didn't even have to juggle courses or think about a major. There was only one elective I had to choose. But that was fine with my mother who thought girls of seventeen were incapable of making intelligent decisions at that young an age.

In junior college I didn't have to make decisions about course curriculum. The two-year Catholic girls college offered a "one curriculum fits all" program of study leading to an AA degree in liberal arts. The few electives offered included the freshman year choice between art and shorthand. I chose shorthand because my mother said I could always put fast note-taking skills to use, whether in a classroom taking lecture notes or in an office taking letters and memos.

When Dr. Long and I sat down with a guidance counselor who was assigned to work the new student registration line, I was nervous about what to say to her and didn't even know what I should be asking. I had never dealt with a guidance counselor before and just didn't know what her function was or how she could help me. I didn't know B.S. from B.A. majors and minors only referred to baseball leagues, as far as I was concerned. I was shocked to find out that the university had a course catalog almost as thick as the Sears catalog.

Dr. Long, thank God, spoke up and explained my situation. She said I was a returning student who had been working for the government for close to thirty years, had some previous college credits, and had earned well over forty CEUs (Continuing Education Units) from a host of job related seminars. I proudly pulled out my page and a half long list of seminar titles to show the advisor.

The advisor looked over my transcript and training records. After noting that most of my education was related to business and operations of the government, she suggested that I seek a degree either in Business Management or in

Management Studies. I chose Management Studies because it didn't require a course in dreaded statistics.

After suggesting a major, the advisor wielded the first major blow to my hope of getting a degree in a short time. She said that none of the thirty or so work related seminars for which I had certificates of completion would be accepted for transfer credit; they were the products of contract vendors or were taught by government personnel and unaccredited. I didn't cry, but I sure felt like it . There went my belief that all the work I put into those courses would contribute some day toward a degree. Continuing education units (CEUs), the advisor explained, are really worthless when it comes to a degree even though they have a direct knowledge value at work. (Another myth shot down.) I felt the same way I did when the Catholic church said St. Christopher was not a saint.

I still had hope that, by some miracle, I could still get a degree if I could just get into the rhythm of classes, studying, writing papers, studying for exams, and finding my way around the campus. Looking around the room while the advisor looked up degree requirements for a B.S. in Management Studies, I saw lots of other "adult" students registering. They all looked just like ordinary people, with ordinary occupations, with ordinary families to take care of, and ordinary kids tagging along with them as they filled out papers and stood in lines.

After getting the requirements list, I thanked the advisor, asked what I had to do next, and went home to read course descriptions, degree requirements, and find out about student study aid facilities on campus. I returned in a day or two on the last walk-in registration day assigned for people with last names starting with *H*. I brought the list of five required courses the advisor and Dr. Long had written down for my major. I found my own way to the right registration room and located the *G-J* registration line. I filled out the complicated registration form, in duplicate, marking down every course on the required list! I was delighted that none of the five class times overlapped. I never gave a second thought to the course load. I treated registration like an office scheduling problem; all the pieces fit so it would of course work out.

The student volunteer who reviewed my registration for twenty-one credit hours told me as politely as possible that eighteen credit hours was the maximum a new student was allowed. After I successfully completed fifteen credits with a 3.0 GPA, then I could petition for a waiver to take more than eighteen credits.

Four classes totaled eighteen credits because two of the classes were worth six credits a piece. Oh well, I could use one free night a week to study or write papers. I also found out that I only had to attend class for one of my four courses because the other three were "Open Learning" courses. Open Learning means students only go to the first and last class sessions for orientation and the final exam. Other class attendance is optional, but written assignments must be submitted as scheduled in the course syllabus.

I picked four courses from the ones required for my degree major. I signed up for the ones I already knew something about or which I thought I could learn easily, like human resource management, adult years, freshman math, and Carl Sagan's *Cosmos*, which was a fun course that also satisfied the math/science requirement.

By this time I had met an advisor, picked out a major, signed up for required courses, and felt getting a degree was going to be smooth sailing. I was comfortable about my courses. I could certainly write about adult years since I already had many years of practical experience. I knew something about human resource management since I routinely managed people at work and children and household help at home.

My plan was simply to earn a degree so I could apply to graduate school to earn credentials for a second career that I could start working part time before I retire. When I retired from my present job, I would switch full time to the second career. All I needed for my degree was eighty credit hours because I had gotten twenty-six credits ten years ago for experiential learning. Any grade of *C* or better would give me credit. It didn't make a whole lot of difference whether I earned high or average grades. Blue, red, or white credit chips would be counted toward the 120 total that I needed.

Because it had been over twenty-five years since I was in junior college, I really didn't know what to expect at adult, night school, part-time university classes. I was naive, anxious, scared, slow to get started, and too casual. I thought adult education would be pretty much the same as junior college where the teachers taught, explained, and reviewed everything their students needed to know in order to pass the classes, which were only forty-five minutes long. I bought the required text books and merrily went to the first class for each course. The next week, without a thought for the consequences to my studies, I left for a pre-scheduled two-week skiing vacation with my daughter in Europe. I returned to the shock that I had missed six hours of required classroom lecture and two integral video presentations in the science class. I had also missed the valuable class discussions in my optional attendance open learning classes. I almost gave up when I realized that my first batch of papers was due the following week, and I hadn't read even one chapter. I had been too busy reading European guide books and ski maps to open any of the 50 lbs of text books I had lugged with me.

I quickly got my act together, turned off all outside interference—the TV, telephone, church choir—and explained to friends that I was out of circulation until the end of the spring semester in mid-April.

But it was hard to change life styles. I was used to weekend trips to local ski resorts, visiting my mother if the skiing was bad, shopping the malls, and finding other ways to procrastinate from burdensome responsibilities. One weekend when I should have been working on a twenty-page paper, I arranged a lunch date with my sister, called a friend to help change the oil in my car, and wasted the whole day Saturday. On Sunday, I forced myself to work at my personal computer until after midnight.

That weekend taught me a valuable lesson to which I credit my success in getting my degree in less than a year and still having friends, family, and a life. That lesson is simply that when papers were due, I did them a little at a time but found time to work on them every day. When chapters needed to be read, I read them a little at a time, but I read them every day.

I needed more study time but didn't seem to have any more time available out of the usual twenty-four hour day. I carefully analyzed my entire day. I looked at every minute from get-up to flop-down. I drove to work; I had almost an hour at lunch; I had a break after work from one to four hours before class; I had every Friday night and all day on Saturday and Sunday free; and I had optional free time if choosing not to go to open learning classes.

To scrounge study time, I changed from driving to work to taking the bus and subway so that I could read, review, or highlight notes, or study for an exam while commuting. I switched from eating lunch with educationally non-nutritious coworkers to eating with a healthy text. I often chose things for lunch that I could eat with one hand so that I could turn pages with the other. I stayed at my desk after work to study because it was a quiet environment where I could read and prepare assignments without the interruptions I had at home. I used the computer center at the university to work on assignments after class. Weekends were reserved for researching and writing major papers on the schedule I worked out.

My first set of mid-term exams was a humongous emotional crisis. I asked almost everyone about their experiences taking real-life college exams. I wanted to know what I should expect; how I should prepare; how much did I have to know about the details of the subject; what if I forgot everything; what about the two weeks when I was in Europe and didn't get the class notes? I went to the first exam scared stiff. I almost lost all composure when I noticed the other students taking out lots of nice clean notebook paper to write their examination answers. I managed to find a broken, dull pencil stub in the bottom of my backpack. I didn't know I was supposed to bring my own paper, so I hastily borrowed a couple of sheets. Then, unnerved, I started reading the exam essay questions.

I barely knew what the questions were asking, let alone

enough additional information to develop five out of seven "accurate and complete" responses. I asked for additional time after working on the exam for nearly two and a half hours. The professor and I were the only ones left. I felt totally dumb. All the other students had long since finished their probably perfect answers while I sat there sweating out every sentence. Finding that I still had one question to answer, he let me have a few more minutes. In tears I handed him my messily written, erased, and scratched out sheets of paper because I was dead certain that I had flunked. The memories from junior college failures still stung. I drove home hysterically wailing about why was I doing this to myself again. Why was I tormenting myself with education? My efforts were all futile; I was the failure my mother told me I was. I cried so hard and had such a sleepless night that I couldn't go to work the next day. It was just as well, since I had to try to study for that night's torture, the science exam. I really hadn't read any of the *Cosmos* text book yet. The next day, starting with coffee at dawn, I frantically read, skimmed, and highlighted each chapter finishing just in time to get to the exam. I had no better feelings about taking this second exam, except that I did remember to bring two sharpened pencils and lots of nice clean notebook paper!

I soothed myself with the thought that these exams were only the mid-terms. If I really did fail a mid-term, I could somehow magically change an *F* into a *C* for credit by the end of the semester, but only if I buckled down right away. I agonized for two long weeks waiting for my exam grades. In the first, hysteria-producing exam, I got a *B*; in the second, I got a *C*. Although not thrilled with my performance, I was pleased since I had only read the science text the day of the exam. Furthermore, by missing class to go skiing, I decreased my chances of getting an *A* on an essay exam. Professors irritated by no-show students are less inclined to grade favorably.

I had learned a new lesson. To get good grades, I should study in advance and not wait until the week or day of an exam. I should also plan my activities so as not to miss class.

I finished the spring semester, passed all my final exams without further tears or trauma, and had eighteen more credits on my transcript bringing the total to fifty-eight.

During the spring semester, I found out from my advisor about earning credit by taking examinations through CLEP, the College Level Examination Program, and ACT/PEP, the American College Testing's Proficiency Examination Program. I could earn up to an unbelievable sixty credits, which would count toward a degree exactly the same as classroom credits. CLEP credits would be entered on my transcript by course title only, no grade. If I failed a CLEP exam, no record of the attempted credit would be recorded.

Credit by examination was a great deal! It was a fast and inexpensive way to earn credit. In an hour and a half I could earn from three to six credits simply by passing a multiple choice exam that cost under forty dollars to take. All I had to do was learn enough about the subject to pass because the exams are only graded pass/fail. I got information from the university's adult education center about what subject exams were offered, which ones Maryland University would accept, since some schools exclude language or other specific exams, and finally, where I could take the exams in addition to those offered at Maryland.

I signed up right away to take two exams at Maryland in June. I would have started taking the CLEPs sooner, but I misunderstood Maryland's policy about credit by exam. I incorrectly thought they wouldn't let me take CLEP exams until after I'd gotten fifteen regular classroom credits. I could have taken the CLEPs and ACTs at any time, even before I registered. The CLEP credits just couldn't go on my transcript until after I finished fifteen classroom credits.

In order to graduate in August, I figured I had to earn thirty-six credits by exam out of the sixty-two that I still needed. I circled about ten exam titles from the list of fifty-five that I thought I might be able to pass with some studying. Only two exams are allowed on the same testing day. I scheduled four days to take eight tests to earn thirty-six credits. Then I got the bad news. Maryland suspended giving

CLEP exams from June until the beginning of the fall semester. But I found out some good news. There were several other colleges in the general area that would be giving the CLEP exams throughout the summer. ACT-PEP exams had separate testing dates and locations. Some places (farther away), I could get to by leaving on Friday night for a Saturday morning exam. I called all the testing colleges and made a list of their test dates to see which ones I could fit with my schedule of classes for the summer semester.

My examination plan was to take four exams in June and four in July. I was saving the month of August to take substitute exams for any I might fail. If I wanted to retake a failed test instead of substituting another test, I would have had to wait three months before being allow to retest.

CLEP requires registration for an exam four weeks in advance. I made good use of the overnight mail service more than once. One test date was closer than the required four weeks away. Instead of throwing up my hands, I called the college test center, explained my situation, and begged for help. They were able to schedule the test because the test I wanted to take was already at the testing site and didn't have to be mailed out by the testing service.

Meanwhile, needing a final twenty-six classroom credits, I registered for eight classes offered in the summer semester. Twenty-six credits were the difference between the 58 credits I had at the end of the spring semester, the 36 credits I planned to earn by examination, and the 120 credits required for my degree.

I was really lucky to find two single weekend courses worth one credit each that would both fit my Saturday schedule and also fit my course requirements. I also was lucky to find four open learning courses that totaled eighteen credits. And lastly, I found a course in the second term of the semester that exactly matched the day and time of a course when I would finish the first term. I drove to the four corners of Washington's suburbs to get to all eight classes, as many as eighty miles a day and three hundred miles a week.

Because I had almost no prior knowledge in most of the

CLEP subject exams I had signed up for, I bought or borrowed books from friends, relatives, and libraries. The guide books for CLEP exams provided a suggested list of texts listed by subject exam. This was much cheaper than laying out hundreds for all the books required by classroom courses.

My first two CLEP exams were Freshman English and Computers and Data Processing. I had taken a non-credit class on computers at work a couple of years back, so I reviewed my old course material to transform an otherwise worthless course into three more credits. I was soaring when I came out of those first two exams. It's almost impossible for a native speaker of English to fail the Freshman English exam. My writing experience at work also helped me pass with ease.

I successfully passed six of the first eight exams and added up twenty-four more credits. Two I didn't pass were exams that couldn't be studied for in a week or two, such as American Literature, which required extensive knowledge gained only by having read volumes of novels by American authors, and I was never much of a reader.

I wrote the testing service asking to withdraw and get a refund for an exam; I realized a week before the test date that I simply didn't know enough about "production management" to pass the exam. I picked out two substitute exams worth six credits each that I could take in August. Because I only passed one, I was six credits short and had to find either another exam for six credits or two exams for three credits each, which I could take in October, the next testing date. I passed in October, completing the thirty-six credits by examination, which I planned and needed for my degree. I was two months behind my schedule for an August graduation, but still in record time.

In all, I earned thirty-six credits by passing nine exams. Those 36 credits, more than a year's worth of conventional classroom time, cost under $350 total!

All along, I tried to pick CLEP exams that overlapped and shared the same base of knowledge, such as Psychology and Educational Psychology, Human Growth and Develop-

ment and Sociology. Analysis and Interpretation of Literature and English Literature also overlapped substantially,
sharing the same set of terms and frames of reference.

Until my advisor reviewed my curriculum to determine
if all degree requirements had been met for graduation, I
didn't find out that I had a problem receiving credit for the
upper level exam, Human Growth and Development, which
I unwittingly took before taking the lower level exam in the
same discipline, Introduction to Psychology. I received the
credits only after writing to petition the Dean of Student
Services for the credits. The road to 120 credits was not
without other potholes, rocks, detours, and near disasters.
Another near major setback was having to get a special
exemption to take more than six credits by examination
during the final thirty hours of classroom credit. It means that
they don't want seniors to fool around for three years and then
pack their transcript full of exam credits in their final two
semesters.

But, in my case, I was only going to be a two-semester
student. I won my petition for exam credit. Not understanding that I could have taken the CLEP and ACT-PEP exams
during or before the spring semester, instead of waiting until
my final semester/thirty credit hours, I came close to ruining
my plan for a degree altogether.

I also had to petition for a waiver of the maximum
twenty-one classroom credits a student is allowed to take
during one semester. I had assumed, obviously incorrectly,
that after I'd received better than the minimum 3.0 GPA
average for my first fifteen classroom hours, I could register
for any number of credits. I didn't find out until standing in
front of the registration table for the summer semester that
twenty-one credits a semester is their absolute maximum.

I was very sure I could handle the twenty-six credits I'd
selected. Two credits would take up just a couple of weekends; six credits were sequential courses in Term I and Term
II; and the remaining eighteen credits were three open learning classes. I just had to speak to the Dean of Student Services
to explain my plan and to convince her I could handle such a
seemingly enormous load. She had to write out five waivers

and send them to each of my professors with a special notation that papers were not to be accepted from me past their set due dates. I was getting weary of waivers by this time.

Many of the problems I encountered were due to my lack of information, miscommunication, or misunderstanding of university rules. One of the most difficult problems I encountered occurred when I changed the initial curriculum plan developed by my advisor. I innocently substituted two CLEP exams for one six-credit work-study project without consulting her. This was a monumental no-no and a very near disaster because the change did not have approval and did not match the official curriculum. Yes, I had to write another petition that resulted in yet another waiver. I wrote so many petitions that I feel qualified to teach a special class in "Petitions and Waivers 101" or "Overcoming Bureaucratic Obstacles to a Degree."

I have never quite been able to accept a negative response or a "you can't do that" without first trying to figure out some other way to get or do what I want to do. This philosophy has gotten me further along than if I were meek and accepting. Without petitions, waivers, questioning, and persistence, I never could have gotten my degree in less than one year.

My best personal advice for returning to college is first of all to stay in close communication with the assigned academic advisor. Try to be friendly; at least always be cordial, respectful, and considerate. He or she is the key to information you need. You should verify and re-verify all of your assumptions. Remember that by asking a lot of questions of a lot of people you will get a lot of different answers. Only the academic advisor has the right answers. Get answers in writing when they are critical.

A second bit of advice is to find out about and use all available student assistance facilities, like the student computer center, especially when you are preparing written material.

My self-confidence soared after I realized, little by little, that I was smarter than I had given myself credit for. Without breaking into a sweat, I found that I had far more than enough ability and study skills to sprint to a degree in college at night and on weekends with other adult learners.

I didn't feel awkward because I was older than the other students in my classes. I was in the middle of the age range and found age didn't make a difference anyhow. I had the understanding of my teachers when it came to due dates or needing to call them at home or work to get help. I felt comfortable knowing they were part-time teachers with other full-time jobs who sincerely wanted their students to succeed.

One year to YOUR college degree is possible. Go for it!

CHAPTER 2
WHAT'S YOUR EXCUSE?

Let's be honest. If a local university were giving out college degrees for one day only at no charge, you and thousands of other people like yourself would line up to get one. The short-term and long-term benefits of a degree are obvious to every one, especially anyone who has had to get a job without a college degree. The vast majority of jobs advertised as vacant require a college degree, even though it may not even be necessary to perform the job. Even if a job does not require a degree, employers are more likely to hire someone with a degree over someone without a degree, assuming—rightly or wrongly—that they are harder working, brighter, and more mature than someone without college credentials.

Yet, in spite of these facts, you haven't found the motivation to return to school. You've toyed with the idea, you may have even started and stopped a few times, but you haven't finished. What's your excuse?

The following eight people have also toyed with the idea of going back to college. Some need 120 credits to earn a degree, while others need less than one year. Each would like to earn a college degree and each has a different, but common, excuse. With which one of these true stories do you identify? Do you think their stories are valid?

"It Will Take Too Long"

After graduating from high school with above average grades, Kathy started college at the local community college. Living at home with her mother and step-father, tension rose, and after one year, she left home and temporarily abandoned her educational goals. At twenty-three Kathy met and married an air force private. Her dream of returning to school was waylaid as she followed her husband from one military base to another, never staying in one place long enough to seriously get involved in school. Within a year, Kathy was expecting a baby. Joyful about the birth of their baby, she was nevertheless disappointed now that school seemed even further away.

This year Kathy celebrated her thirtieth birthday. Recently divorced, she moved back home. Her two children, ages six and four, also live with her. Kathy works full time in the purchasing department of a large hospital where her younger child is enrolled in the daycare center. In the ten years since she left home, there have been difficult times. Kathy, forced by necessity to take a variety of jobs, fully appreciates the importance of a college degree. But, faced with family and work responsibilities as a single parent, she doesn't know how she is going to find the time to get her degree. No family members have volunteered to watch her children in the evening, and even if she could find an evening babysitter, Kathy thinks a degree would take too long.

It takes 120 semester credits to earn a college degree. Kathy already has thirty credits from her one year of community college. If she took one three-credit course each semester, she would earn six credits a year. At that rate it would take her fifteen years to earn her college degree. Kathy would be forty-five-years-old and her two children would be in college. If Kathy doubled that course load and took six credits a semester, the average load for an adult student, she could earn twelve credits per year and it would take her just seven and a half years to earn her degree. That's still a long, long time to have to struggle with work, school, and family. Yet, if she took six credits each semester plus six credits during the summer, she would earn eighteen credits a year and her degree in five years. No wonder Kathy is discouraged.

"I've Been Away from School Too Long"

Barbara is a youthful fifty-five. The mother of three daughters, she quit work when her first daughter, Ann, was born. Barbara was a mother and homemaker until her youngest daughter, Nancy, entered high school. Bored at home, Barbara got a job at a local private school as a teacher's aide. Her years of experience as a first-rate mother and grandmother made her a valuable asset to the school. As an aide, Barbara assisted a variety of licensed teachers. Her wisdom and experience helped her to quickly learn how to organize a classroom like a professional even though she didn't have a single college credit.

Being an aide, Barbara often felt frustrated because she frequently knew more than the twenty-two-year-old teachers she was assigned to assist. Recognizing her talent and skill, the headmistress put her in charge of her own classroom of three-year-olds. Technically still an aide because she did not have a college degree and was not licensed as a pre-school educator, Barbara was paid a fraction of a regular teacher's salary even though she had the same responsibilities. Although Barbara loved working with young children, she felt she didn't have the respect of the other teachers, who were the ages of her own children, nor did she feel part of the faculty. The lack of a degree also made her more tentative about everything. If she was late for work once, she was afraid she would get fired. Her greatest fear was that the parents of the preschoolers would discover that she was an impostor.

Barbara often thinks about going back to school. She knows she has a real talent for working with children and wishes she had pursued her degree in teaching when she was younger. Yet, she doesn't take the idea of going back to college full-time seriously, even though she genuinely desires a degree. Barbara is afraid that she doesn't have what it takes to get a degree today.

Barbara falsely thinks that because she's older, it will be harder for her to succeed in the courses she would have to take; that, somehow, she has forgotten how to study; that she's lost the skills needed to be a good student. In fact, just the opposite is true. Barbara's years of work experience have given her background knowledge and skills that can help her succeed in school.

Barbara's memory may not be what it used to be, but the years she has spent in the workforce have given her a lot of skills that will help her as a student. Her years of working in a pre-school have taught her much about children and about education. She has acquired valuable knowledge that will help her in both the psychology and education courses necessary for a degree.

Barbara is also more disciplined than a traditional student. Because she's had to get up for work, complete projects on time, manage time between work and home responsibilities, Barbara has learned how to manage and use time wisely. Not likely to get distracted by a new boyfriend, pledging a sorority, or feeling homesick, Barbara would be a disciplined student.

Barbara would also be a committed student. If Barbara chooses to go back to school, it would be because it is something she wants to do rather than because her parents sent her, or her friends were all doing it. Adult students usually pay for their own education, and most arrange financing. Younger students typically rely on their parents to handle the college bills from savings or signing for educational loans.

"It's Impossible to Manage School, Work, and Home"

The daughter of working class parents, Bonnie grew up in New York City. Because of the scarcity of money rather than her scholastic ability, college was never in her plans. Her parents valued a good job with a stable institution such as the telephone company, transit authority, or a bank, "so you don't have to worry where your next meal is coming from." After high school she married a traditional Italian husband who believed that a woman's place is at home taking care of him and his children. Bonnie complied and raised three children.

When her husband's upward mobility led to life in the suburbs, Bonnie's horizons expanded, and she realized a college degree was within her reach. She raised the issue of returning to school with her husband who could now easily afford the tuition. Less than supportive, he argued, "The children need you," or "I want you to be home when I come home from work. Is that too much to ask?" Even when her children were in high school, Bonnie's husband discouraged her from returning to school. Threatened by the fact that he did not have a degree, the thought that she might earn one upset him.

Nancy, also dissuaded by home responsibilities, believes it's impossible to manage work, home, school, and parenting responsibilities. The single mother of two young children, her schedule has her rushing home from work to be with her eight- and ten-year-old daughters. She isn't comfortable leaving them alone during the time they are home from school until she can get home from work. When pressed to return to school by her parents, Nancy argues, "How can I manage cooking, cleaning, and the other chores of running a home and, at the same time, attend classes, do hours of homework, write research papers, study for exams, and help my daughters with their homework?"

"I Can't Afford College"

When she was eighteen, Sam's parents sent her to a prestigious state college. Near the end of her freshman year, she dropped out, earning only six credits for a whole year's effort. After a less than stellar college performance, Sam worked in her father's flower shop for three years. Recently she got a job as a secretary with a law firm. Although she finds the clerical job boring, she does receive health care benefits and makes double the salary she earned at the flower shop.

With test scores in the 99th percentile, Sam is definitely college material. When asked why she doesn't go back to college, her repeated excuse is "I can't afford it." Sam could live with her mom instead of sharing a house and its expenses with three friends. Most of her income goes to basic living expenses for food, transportation, clothing, rent, and utilities. In her new job, Sam hopes to be able to save enough money to pay for school in a few years.

Sam uses the cost of college as an excuse for not returning to school now. If she were seriously interested in school, she could apply to college and contact the financial aid office for assistance.

"I'm Not Sure a Degree Is Worth the Effort"

At thirty-nine, Jo Ann would like to have her degree, but she doesn't think a degree is worth the effort. She claims that as an artist, her portfolio is as important as a college degree. Occasionally, when business is bad, she'll reluctantly admit a college degree could help her get more opportunities to present her portfolio. Jo Ann also knows that with a college degree a lot of difficult times could have been avoided.

When Jo Ann couldn't sell enough artwork to pay her bills, she would teach art in the after-school program at the YMCA or work as an art teacher in a private school. These jobs, even though they were personally rewarding, only paid between five and eight dollars an hour and allowed her to work only three or four hours a day.

A degree would have allowed Jo Ann to apply for a position teaching art in the public school system where she could earn thirty thousand dollars a year plus benefits. A licensed teacher has a tenured position with job stability, automatic salary increases, and a higher marketability. Being an hourly employee in a small, private school, Jo Ann earns a fraction of what her public school counterparts receive for doing the exact same work. Even if she stayed at the same job, with a degree she would qualify for an immediate raise plus substantial employee benefits.

With her degree, Jo Ann would be a more highly qualified and marketable employee. She could look for a job both in the public and in the private school sectors, rather than feeling limited to the few private schools in her area. If she had a problem at her current job, it would make it easier for her to find another one.

Without official credentials, Jo Ann has no opportunity for professional advancement. She could not, for instance, be promoted to the head of the art department, principal, or even assistant principal of the school. In schools and in other work places, credentials are critical to professional advancement.

Jo Ann would like to make a career change. She would like to work as a commercial artist rather than as a pseudo art teacher. If she earned a degree in commercial art, it would compensate for her lack of work experience in that area.

"College Will Ruin My Social Life"

David is a twenty-eight-year-old salesman for a national cosmetics firm. His job allows him extensive travel on the company's expense account. Although he has three years of college under his belt, a college degree would help him advance into a management position. He is often distracted by the lifestyle his job affords. David dates heavily and is only willing to spare one evening a week for school responsibilities.

Going back to school often means postponing gratification. Dating, eating out, and a life of traveling all bring David immediate pleasure. Being a college student requires making decisions about activities. College takes some amount of time; and generally the most time consuming recreational activities are the first to be eliminated.

Resources for More Information

Psychological and Physical Barriers to Returning to School

Nieves, Luis, Psy.D. *Coping in College: Successful Strategies.* Princeton, NJ: Education Testing Service, 1984.

Coping in College gives sound advice for coping with

study, anxiety, depression, conflict, and test-taking. Every chapter contains many self-help charts, worksheets, checklists, schedules, exercises, and activities.

O'Neill, Joseph P. *Corporate Tuition Aid Programs: A Directory of College Financial Aid for Employees at America's Largest Corporations,* 2d ed. Princeton: Conference of University Press, 1986.

The Corporate Tuition Aid Program has concise charts, detail policies, and procedures on tuition benefits for 650 of the Fortune 1000 companies. Explains which employees are eligible, how long they must be employed, what percent of tuition costs are paid by the company, when the employee will be reimbursed, and what types of courses are included.

Pauk, Walter *How to Study in College.* Boston: Houghton Mifflin, 1989.

A concise, comprehensive guide, How to Study in College offers proven methods that can help anyone learn how to learn. It has detailed sections on reading and understanding literature, poetry, math, law, and the sciences. It shows how to get the most from your reading, how to research reports, how to generally keep up with a field of interest or study without great investment of time and money.

Walter, Tim and Al Siebert *Student Success: How to Succeed in College and Still Have Time for Your Friends,* 5th ed. Chicago: Holt, Rinehart & Winston, Inc., 1990.

Student Success helps students get good grades and enjoy a social life by telling students how to learn more in less time. It provides the student with specific, practical study skills that show how to quickly gain an understanding of the material in each course to get good grades. *Student Success* describes how to have time to play sports, do things with friends, socialize, date, watch TV, go to movies, or keep up a fitness program. It includes self help activities and charts.

CHAPTER 3
COLLEGE IN THE
FAST LANE

Classroom earned college credits are expensive in time, money, and effort, but attending class is not the only way to earn college credit. By earning college credit in a variety of ways and keeping conventional classroom credits to a minimum, the **One Year to a College Degree Program** gives you a quick and easy way to earn a legitimate bachelor's degree. If you are diligent, have some college, have rich life experiences, and have on-the-job learning, you don't have to spend years earning your degree. Using a combination of previous college credit, life experience credit, credits earned by examination for previous knowledge, credits earned for projects carried out at work, and an intensive study year, you can earn your college degree in one year.

How It's Done

You can earn your degree in one year by following a simple six-step program. The object of the program is to accumulate 120 credits from a variety of non-traditional methods in one year. Earning credit solely from traditional methods is overly time consuming and quite expensive.

Step One: Select a College

Selecting the right college is the single most important step in successfully earning your degree in one year. The *right* college is not the closest, cheapest, or the easiest, but rather the college that has the programs in place that will allow you to earn your degree quickly and easily. You need a school that will award college credit for life experience, accept transfer credit for courses you've taken at other colleges and universities, accept credit earned by examination, and allow credits to be earned via cooperative education or independent study programs. If your area college has all these programs, you are well on your way to being able to earn your degree in one year. In order to help you choose the right college, a step-by-step **College Evaluation Guide** is contained in chapter 9. It will help you evaluate the colleges in your area according to these and a number of other criteria.

Step Two: Transfer Previous College Credits

After you've selected a college, it's time to start accumulating credits. Before you start earning new credits, you need to determine what credits you might already have. The first place to look is previous college experience. If you attended college before, even if only for one semester, or took a few evening classes at the local community college, the credits you earned should be transferred. Every credit you already have is one less credit you must earn.

Besides credits from college courses, you may be able to obtain credit for classes you took at work, while in the military, or for pleasure. Evaluate all of these non-college courses as possible sources of credit. In order to get an idea of how many college credits you may have earned, ask an admissions officer at the college you selected to conduct a preliminary evaluation of all of your previous college and non-college coursework.

Step Three: Apply for Life Experience Credit

Most colleges now recognize and award credit for education gained from work or volunteer experiences. You can get credits for a variety of activities such as coaching a sports team, campaigning for a political candidate, teaching Sunday school, designing a computer application, drawing, or managing a cottage business. Colleges admit that adults gain college-level learning from these and hundreds of other activities. Consequently, any activity that can be related to knowledge taught in college is eligible for life experience credit.

Earning life experience credit involves the preparation of a portfolio. The portfolio is your way of proving both what you've done and what you've learned. The first section of the portfolio, the personal narrative, is a description of who you are and what you've done. The second section is a detailed description of the courses for which you want credit and an itemized justification to support your proposal.

If you're interested in earning life experience credit, contact the college or university you will be attending. Since experiential learning programs have different names at different colleges, don't get discouraged if you run into a few roadblocks in finding the right office. Possible places to look include the Assessment of Prior Learning Office, Portfolio Assessment Office, Experiential Learning Office, or Adult Education Office.

Step Four: Obtain Credit by Examination

Over twenty-five hundred colleges and universities award college credit to students for passing nationally standardized examinations. These exams give you a chance to prove what you've learned on your own while at work, living in a foreign country, reading independently, taking non-credit courses, or through any other activities. The advantages of receiving credit by examination are huge cost savings and the rapid accumulation of credit. There are no classes to attend or papers to write. In most cases you only have to pass a ninety-minute multiple choice exam to earn from three to six credits.

The two major testing programs are the College Level Equivalency Program (CLEP) administered by the College Board and the Proficiency Examination Program (PEP) administered by the American College Testing Program. These programs test student competency in a wide variety of areas including English, Math, Computer Science, Social Studies, Science, Psychology, Education, Foreign Language, Business, and Nursing.

To earn credit by examination, contact both the CLEP

and PEP programs. Their addresses are in chapter 5 with more information about each program. Obtain the most recent list of exam titles, testing dates, and locations. Sign up for those exams that you have natural talents for or a strong background in.

Step Five: Apply for Cooperative Education Credits and Independent Study Credits

Most colleges have programs that will award credit for learning gained through specific on-the-job experience, while working under the supervision of a faculty member. These cooperative education programs usually involve some employment-related project that demonstrates the acquisition of new knowledge. In a cooperative education program, the time you spend on the job is your class time; and the learning you acquire as part of your job is the course content. Cooperative education programs integrate theory with on-the-job learning.

Cooperative education programs are an easy way to earn credits. There are no exams to take, books to read, or classes to attend. Traditional requirements for a cooperative education program include occasional meetings with a faculty advisor and a written report that describes the project and what was learned. Colleges set limits on the number of cooperative education programs you can earn both per semester and during your entire academic career. The traditional limit is no more than six credits a semester with a maximum of fifteen credits total. With an easy project, these can be six easy credits. To earn cooperative education credits, contact the Cooperative Education Office at your college or university.

Independent study projects are another way to earn credits without attending class. During an independent study project, you design your own course with the assistance of a faculty member. You decide on the course objectives, content, activities, and assignments. Tailor made to meet your needs, abilities, and interests, independent study projects are an effortless way to earn college credits. If you are interested in earning independent study credits, think of an idea and find a faculty member in the appropriate area to work with you. Your college or public library has books that can help you develop an independent study topic.

Step Six: Take Regular College Credits

After credits from every other possible source are gathered together, conventional courses are taken. You'll want to select college courses that fulfill your degree requirements quickly and integrate any previous creditable work. College courses that follow the traditional format of meeting three times a week are avoided; courses that follow more flexible class scheduling are pursued. Weekend classes, televised classes, open learning classes, and correspondence classes are all given preference. Courses that award a high number of credits are given preference over lower credit courses. Selecting college courses is done with great care. Your program of study outlines all the additional courses you'll need to earn a degree in your major.

One Hundred Twenty Credits

By putting these six steps together, you reasonably can expect to earn your college degree in a year. The credits from these five sources can add up quickly to 120 credits in one year. The number and combination of transfer credits, life experience credits, examination credits, cooperative education credits, and course credits will differ from student to student. There is no magic combination since students differ in the number of transfer credits they start with, the variety and depth of their life experience, their ability to earn credit by examination, and the suitability of their job to cooperative education projects.

Colleges differ in their policies and graduation requirements, which will impact the program you design. Some have liberal transfer credit policies; others are highly restrictive in the number of credits and type of credit they will accept. Some schools allow students to earn credits via portfolio assessment, others don't. Most schools accept examination

credits, but some do not. Some have cooperative education
programs, while others don't. The programs a school has, or
more importantly doesn't have, will shape the degree program a student develops.

These individual and institutional differences mean that
the one year to a degree program will be unique for each
student. Here are five sample ways a student could earn the
required 120 credits for graduation.

SAMPLE PROGRAM A

Transfer Credit	30 credits
Life Experience Credit	30 credits
Credit by Examination	30 credits
Cooperative Education Credit	15 credits
Coursework	15 credits
TOTAL CREDITS	120 credits

Analysis: Sample Program A is an example of a bal-
anced program. Credits are earned in each of the five areas.
To earn a degree from their school, most colleges require
their students to earn a minimum of thirty credits there. Credits earned by examination and by portfolio assessment are
considered transfer credits and don't count toward the thirty
credit minimum. However, the fifteen credits earned from
traditional college coursework and the fifteen credits from
cooperative education do count as campus earned credits.
These fifteen cooperative education credits could actually
be a combination of cooperative education credits and independent study credits.

SAMPLE PROGRAM B

Transfer Credit	0 credit
Life Experience Credit	30 credits
Credit by Examination	30 credits
Cooperative Education Credit	15 credits
Coursework	45 credits
TOTAL CREDITS	120 credits

Analysis: Although most students who return to college have at least thirty college credits, some students have no transfer credits at all. This is an example of a program for such a student. It may be harder to earn a degree in exactly one year without transfer credit, but an ambitious student can easily earn a degree in less than two years.

If a student earns less than the desired number of credits in one category, the other categories can make up the difference. For example, in sample Program B, more traditional courses were taken to compensate for the lack of transfer credits. Notice that in this program and in Program D, sixty credits are taken at the selected school. Many colleges and universities require students to earn a minimum of sixty credits as a registered student at that school before being eligible for a degree from that institution regardless of the total number of credits accumulated. The **One Year to a College Degree Program** will work at schools that have a sixty credit minimum, although it is highly advisable that you avoid such schools since they greatly reduce program flexibility and the speed at which you can earn your degree.

SAMPLE PROGRAM C

Transfer Credit	60 credits
Life Experience Credit	0 credit
Credit by Examination	20 credits
Cooperative Education Credit	10 credits
Coursework	<u>30 credits</u>
TOTAL CREDIT	120 credits

Analysis: This is a sample program for a student with extensive transfer credits. In this program there are no life experience credits. The student hasn't had a chance to do much that would earn life experience credit, or the school the student is attending doesn't award life experience credit. Without the option of life experience, the best way to approach earning the remaining sixty credits is to attempt as many examination credits as possible. Earning examination credits will reduce the number of credits that must be earned by time consuming, traditional coursework. Twenty credits is the normal number of examination credits that should be attempted. The additional forty credits are earned first through a cooperative education project and then from coursework. If two more examinations resulted in six more examination credits, that would reduce the number of needed coursework credits to twenty-four.

SAMPLE PROGRAM D

Transfer Credit	30 credits
Life Experience Credit	30 credits
Credit by Examination	0 credits
Cooperative Education Credit	15 credits
Coursework	45 credits
TOTAL CREDITS	120 credits

Analysis: This program illustrates a student with a year's worth of transferable credit along with rich life experiences that are expected to earn thirty credits through evaluation of the documented portfolio. Because of degree requirements, there are no CLEP or PEP examinations that fit the curriculum which haven't already been credited from coursework. This student can count on earning just fifteen credits from a cooperative education project. The last forty-five credits will come from carefully selected coursework. If fifteen examination credits could be earned, then only thirty credits of traditional coursework would be taken.

SAMPLE PROGRAM E

Transfer Credit	15 credits
Life Experience Credit	30 credits
Credit by Examination	45 credits
Cooperative Education Credit	0 credits
Coursework	30 credits
TOTAL CREDITS	120 credits

Analysis: This program is for the student who has completed a minimum of college work and doesn't have a job that could be the basis of cooperative education credit. However, the time not spent working was spent in a variety of activities such as in community organizations, programs for charity, volunteer work in different areas, and political campaign work. These experiences can earn the maximum life experience credit. The non-working student also has more time to prepare for CLEP and PEP exams and can earn forty-five or more examination credits. The subject areas in which life experience is earned can't duplicate the examination subjects taken. Extensive life experience and examination credit would leave only thirty credits to be earned through coursework. These courses can be conventional classroom courses or unconventional, open learning courses not requiring class attendance.

One Actual Program

An in-depth analysis of Eileen's program of study will show you specifically how it can be done and how to plan your own program.

First, Eileen had to choose a college. She decided on the University of Maryland, University College because it had the flexibility that allowed her to complete her degree in one year.

Prior Learning Programs. The University of Maryland allows students to earn up to thirty credits through EXCEL, their life experience program.

Credit by Examination. The University of Maryland allows students to earn up to sixty credits by examination provided there isn't duplication of other academic credit and the scores earned meet the college cut-off scores. The college accepts credits earned by all three major testing organizations: the College Board College Level Examination Program (CLEP), USAFI/DANTES examinations, and the American College Testing/Proficiency Examination Program (ACT/PEP). At the University of Maryland, credits earned by examination can be used to satisfy core, major, minor, or elective requirements.

Transfer Credits. The University of Maryland accepts

up to ninety transfer credits. They accept transfer credits from other colleges and universities, junior and community colleges, technical and vocational schools, correspondence courses, as well as approved educational experiences in the armed forces.

Minimal Core Requirements. The core at the University of Maryland is only thirty credits and provides students with maximum flexibility. Students are required to take three communications courses, one of which is Freshman English, two social science courses, two humanities courses, and three courses in math and/or natural science, one of which is a math course.

Open Learning Courses. Open Learning courses allow students to earn college credit via non-traditional formats. Students can earn college credit in courses where class attendance is optional except for an introductory session and final examination, or in classes that are taught over cable television and can be viewed at home.

Convenient Course Scheduling. The University of Maryland caters to adult students. They offer evening, weekend, Saturday, and television courses. University College was also selected because of its large size, which enables it to offer hundreds of courses at every possible hour of the day and night, seven days a week.

Affordable Tuition. As a state-sponsored university, the University of Maryland is able to offer courses at public college tuition rates. Eileen paid only $110 per semester credit hour.

Once Eileen picked a college, she selected a major. She narrowed her choices to a degree in business immediately since she had worked for the federal government in a variety of business and management positions for twenty-seven years. She reasoned that her experience in the government as an administrative assistant, management analyst, budget analyst, and administrative officer would give her a strong base upon which to earn her degree. She planned to use this base to "CLEP" business credits, earn life experience credit, and breeze through courses that overlapped her experience.

After deciding to major in business, she had to choose

between majoring in Business and Management or in Management Studies. Business and Management required thirty-three credits of highly specific courses including two semesters of accounting, economics, and statistics. A primary concentration in Management Studies, on the other hand, required only twenty-one semester hours of management-related courses. The required courses could be selected from any of those offered in the business areas as long as at least fifteen credits were upper level courses.

Obviously Management Studies was the preferred major, especially since very few people would know the difference between her major in Management Studies and the alternative Business and Management once she had her degree.

Eileen earned the 120 credits she needed for graduation four ways: transfer, life experience, examination, and course work. Here, specifically, is how she did it.

TRANSFER CREDITS (20 credits)

Now that she had a college and a major selected, it was up to Eileen to accumulate the 120 credits that met the requirements of her major. The first thing she did was apply for transfer credits. Although she had attended two semesters of junior college, Eileen earned only fourteen transferable credits. Courses in which she earned lower than a C could not be transferred. The university also decided not to give transfer credit for courses in theology because they were taught at a Catholic college and consequently were judged to have a particular religious sect base. She had also taken two courses at The American University, which totaled six additional credits.

The 20 credits Eileen transferred were:

Choral Singing	2 credits
Educational Planning Seminar	3 credits
Introduction to Philosophy	3 credits
Issues, Ideas and Words	3 credits
Philosophy of Man	3 credits
Shorthand	3 credits
U.S. History I	3 credits

LIFE EXPERIENCE CREDITS (20 credits)

In 1980, Eileen made a feeble attempt at earning her degree from the American University. She applied to American University's Life Experience Program, called APEL, Assessment of Prior Experiential Learning, and earned twenty credits for her effort. Now intent on earning her degree at the University of Maryland, she transferred these credits there.

The 20 Life Experience Credits were:

Administrative Politics	3 credits
American Government	3 credits
Bureau Politics	3 credits
Commercial Photography	3 credits
Federal Budget	3 credits
Management and Supervision	3 credits
Recreational Activities	2 credits

CLEP AND ACT/PEP EXAMINATIONS
(36 credits)

Eileen carefully selected the examinations she wanted to take that would provide the maximum amount of credit for the least amount of studying. Eileen also earned credit by choosing course examinations that had a high degree of overlap of knowledge.

The CLEP and ACT/PEP Examinations she passed were:

Analysis and Interpretation of Literature	6 credits
English Literature	6 credits
Introduction to Psychology	3 credits
Educational Psychology	3 credits
Introduction to Sociology	3 credits
Human Growth and Development	3 credits
Introduction to Accounting	6 credits
Freshman English	3 credits
Computers & Data Processing	3 credits

COURSEWORK

Finally, Eileen needed to earn credits by taking regular

courses. She needed 120 credits less 20 from transfer, 20 from life experience, 36 from CLEP and PEP, which left 44 to be earned from traditional classes. She selected courses that awarded high credits and that were offered in an open learning or televised format.

The courses she took were:

OPEN LEARNING—

Adult Years	6 credits
Human Resource Management	6 credits
Strategic Planning	6 credits
Humor in American Society	6 credits
Business Writing	3 credits

TELEVISED—

Math	3 credits
Intro. to Computer-Based Systems	3 credits

REQUIRED CLASS ATTENDANCE—

Writing for Managers	3 credits
Astronomy—Cosmos	3 credits
Theories of Listening	3 credits

ONE-WEEKEND COURSES—

Leisure and Social Transitions	1 credit
Stress Management	1 credit

Now let's look at the whole thing put together. These tables combine a list of both University of Maryland requirements and how Eileen satisfied these requirements. On the left are the university's requirements. In the middle are letters that symbolize how Eileen satisfied the requirement:

TR = Transfer Credit
LE = Life Experience Credit (APEL Program)
EX = Examination Credit (CLEP & PEP)
CO = Cooperative Education Credit
CL = Classwork

On the right is a list of the specific courses Eileen took to satisfy the requirements for a degree in Business Management.

Study Eileen's program of study. In chapter 10 you will learn how to design your own program of study so that you can earn your degree in one year.

Eileen's Program of Study:
General Education Requirements (30 credits):

Comm	TR	LE	**EX**	CO	CL	Fr. English
Comm	TR	LE	EX	CO	**CL**	Listening
Comm	TR	LE	EX	CO	**CL**	Writing/ Mgrs.
SS	TR	**LE**	EX	CO	CL	Admin. Politics
SS	TR	LE	**EX**	CO	CL	Intro./Soci- ology
Human	**TR**	LE	EX	CO	CL	U.S. History I
Human	**TR**	LE	EX	CO	CL	Choral Singing
Math	TR	LE	EX	CO	**CL**	Math 105
Math/NS	TR	LE	EX	CO	**CL**	Astronomy
Math/NS	TR	LE	**EX**	CO	CL	Comp/Data Proc

MAJOR: Management Studies (24 credits)

(Includes any management-related courses from Business Management, Economics, Information Systems Management, Management Studies. At least fifteen of the required twenty-four credits must be in upper level courses.)

TR	LE	EX	CO	**CL**	Comp. Systems
TR	**LE**	EX	CO	CL	Mgt/Supervision
TR	LE	EX	CO	**CL**	Hum Res Mgmt.
TR	LE	EX	CO	**CL**	Hum Res Mgmt.
TR	LE	EX	CO	**CL**	Strat. Planning
TR	LE	EX	CO	**CL**	Strat. Planning
TR	LE	**EX**	CO	CL	Intro. Account
TR	LE	**EX**	CO	CL	Intro. Account

MINOR: Behavioral Science (21 credits)

TR	**LE**	EX	CO	CL	American Govt.
TR	**LE**	EX	CO	CL	Admin. Politics
TR	LE	**EX**	CO	CL	Intro. Psych.
TR	LE	EX	CO	**CL**	Adlt. Cont. & Ch.

TR	LE	EX	CO	**CL**	Adlt. Cont. & Ch.
TR	LE	EX	CO	**CL**	Humor/Am. Soc.
TR	LE	EX	CO	**CL**	Humor/Am. Soc.
TR	LE	**EX**	CO	CL	Human Gro./Dev.

LANGUAGE OR SUBSTITUTION (12 credits)

TR	**LE**	EX	CO	CL	Bureau Politics
TR	**LE**	EX	CO	CL	Federal Budget

ELECTIVES: (33 credits)

TR	LE	**EX**	CO	CL	Intro. Account
TR	LE	**EX**	CO	CL	Intro. Account
TR	**LE**	EX	CO	CL	Comm. Photog.
TR	LE	EX	CO	CL	Educ. Planning
TR	**LE**	EX	CO	CL	Rec. Activities
TR	LE	EX	CO	CL	Shorthand
TR	LE	**EX**	CO	CL	Anal./Int. of Lit.
TR	LE	**EX**	CO	CL	English Lit
TR	LE	**EX**	CO	CL	Educ. Psych.
TR	LE	EX	CO	**CL**	Stress Mgmt.
TR	LE	EX	CO	CL	Phil. of Man
TR	LE	EX	CO	CL	Iss., Ideas/Words
TR	LE	EX	CO	**CL**	Leis./Soc. Trans.

General Guidelines for Following the Program

Now that you know how to earn the 120 credits in one year, here are some general guidelines to provide you with further help.

1. Study the Program. At this point you have an overview of the program, but in order to be successful, you need to understand the program more fully. The remainder of the book explains the **One Year to a College Degree Program** in detail. It provides you with specific strategies, resources, and information necessary to achieve your goal. It tells you how to evaluate your own transcript for credit, how to appeal decisions, where to write for information about testing, and how to get an appointment with an admissions officer. Don't just *read* **One Year to a College Degree**, *study it* and use it as a personal resource manual.

The remaining seven chapters give you step-by-step instructions on how you can realistically earn a bachelor's degree in one year. **Chapter 4** shows you how to earn college credit for life experience. **Chapter 5** tells you how to earn credit by examination. **Chapter 6** provides guidelines for earning transfer credit for college and non-college courses. **Chapter 7** describes how you can use a Cooperative Education Program or an Independent Study Program to earn credit for what you already do at work or at home. **Chapter 8** advises you on how to select college courses that fill remaining degree requirements. **Chapter 9** will help you evaluate colleges before you decide where to apply. **Chapter 10** helps you develop your own program of study.

2. Follow the Steps in Order. The **One Year to a College Degree Program** contains six steps. It is important that you follow these six steps *in order.* You shouldn't sign up for classes before you see what transfer credits you have because you may wind up taking unnecessary classes and earning unusable credits. You shouldn't take CLEP or PEP exams before your portfolio is evaluated for life experience credit because your examination credits may be disallowed if your portfolio is awarded credit for the same learning. You shouldn't start taking classes at the school closest to you before you've evaluated all the schools in your area since the closest school might not have the range of programs or policies that you'll need to get your degree quickly.

3. Plan Ahead. The secret to earning a degree quickly and simply is prior planning. A few hours spent planning and organizing can save you hundreds of hours attending the wrong college, taking difficult or unnecessary courses, or duplicating your efforts. Careful evaluation of your options can save you time and money. Design a program of study before you take a single course.

4. Take Responsibility for Earning Your Degree. No one cares about your degree as much as you do. Consequently, you should take primary responsibility for seeing that you earn it. Don't count on your spouse, children, mother or father, best friend, or academic advisor to do your work for you. Even though these people can be enormously helpful, getting your degree is up to you. Research your options for majors, transfer credits, college choices, and graduation requirements yourself.

   5. Gather Information from Primary Sources. In order to earn your degree in one year, you're going to have to gather a large amount of information. Get that information from primary sources instead of through word of mouth and other informal means. Don't ask your friend if your state university awards or accepts life experience credit. Call the university and get the answer directly from the program office. Don't depend on your friendly advisor to tell you every last detail regarding what you'll need to earn a degree; study the college catalog about your degree program yourself, then ask your advisor to clarify information that you're uncertain about. Secondhand information is dangerous and often represents misinformation. Get firsthand information so that you are sure to base your decisions on correct assumptions.

   6. Stick to It. It's truly possible to earn your degree in one year, but it will take dedication and no doubt some sacrifice on your part. Don't quit. Think of the near-term benefits you will have as well as the many potential far-term benefits for yourself and your family. Being a college-educated adult is your personal achievement and investment, one that can never be taken away and will increase in value over time.

   7. Don't Accept "No" for an Answer. If you ask your advisor whether you can substitute one course for another and the answer is "no," ask someone else who has the authority to say "yes." If you ask your advisor whether you can receive life experience credits and the answer is "no," ask the adult education office or other program office with the power to say "yes."

   Most college faculty members don't know what's going on outside their own department or college. Make it your personal rule to check with at least three different college officials before accepting "no" for an answer.

8. Check, Double Check, and Recheck. In order to ensure that you don't make a costly mistake, check, double check, and recheck everything. Check your degree requirements, major requirements, course offerings, and college rules. Check, double check, and recheck all dates and deadlines. Earning your degree quickly gives you little time to make a mistake or to let something fall through the cracks through no one's fault. Check, double check, and recheck to make sure your credits are being recorded on your transcript, and to make sure you are registered correctly for classes, to make sure your examination credits are ones the college will accept.

9. Find the Quickest Way Possible. The purpose of the **One Year to a College Degree Program** is to help you to earn your degree as quickly as possible. When making decisions, keep this objective in mind. You may enjoy taking a course on Chaucer more than Shakespeare, but if one is worth six credits and the other is worth three, make your decision on credit value rather than on personal preferences. If you want to choose your preference knowing it will cost you time, you can.

Questions about the Program

Even when the program is thoroughly explained, many adults have questions about the program. Here is a list of frequently asked questions and our answers

Q: I've heard of degree mills, does this program earn me a degree from one of them?

A: Degree mills are colleges that grant degrees on a fee basis. These colleges don't have a residency requirement and little or no work is required. The **One Year to a College Degree Program** is not a way to earn a degree from a degree mill, but rather gives students some ways to speed up the process of earning a degree from **nationally recognized, fully accredited colleges and universities.**

Q: Can I use this method to earn a degree from any college?

A: Although some colleges and universities are more suited to this accelerated program than others, the **One Year to a College Degree Program** will help you speed up the process of earning a degree at any college or university. The more flexible the school is in its degree requirements, the quicker you can earn your degree.

Q: Will I earn a bachelor's degree or an associate's degree?

A: The **One Year to a College Degree Program** will help you to earn a conventional four-year bachelor's degree in one year or less. An associate's degree is a two-year degree awarded by a junior or community college.

Q: Will it work for any major?

A: The **One Year to a College Degree Program** is not limited to certain majors; the six steps of the program can be applied to any major. However the less rigid the degree requirements the more quickly you can earn your degree. Professional majors such as business or education generally have more course requirements and take longer to complete. Liberal arts, history, or English majors are less restrictive and so are quicker and easier to finish.

Q: Is it legal?

A: The program as outlined is completely legal. Although most colleges and universities don't promote opportunities for earning a degree at an accelerated rate, the programs that enable students to earn their degree in less than the usual four years are in operation at most universities and colleges throughout the country.

Q: If I don't have any previous college credit, can I still earn my degree in one year?

A: The more college credits you have, the easier it will be for you to earn your degree in one year. Even if you have no previous college experience, it is possible to earn your college degree in one year, but it will take more effort on your part. The fewer number of transferable credits you've earned, the harder you are going to have to work to earn credits in other ways.

Q: Can I earn my degree in less than a year?

A: Every student and situation is different. The speed at which you earn your degree is based on the number of transferable credits you have, the suitability of the college you selected to an accelerated program, and how hard you want to work. All three of these factors are important, but by far the most important is your own motivation.

Q: I want to go to graduate school; will earning my degree in one year hurt my chances of admission?

A: Not at all. The graduate school admissions office will be impressed by the fact that you could complete four years of college work in a single year. On the other hand, the fact that you earned your degree from an accredited school will not guarantee your admission to graduate school. Grades and acceptable admissions test scores are also factors that determine your admission to graduate school. Most universities require a satisfactory score on the Graduate Records Exam (GRE) or the Miller Analogies Test (MAT) as a prerequisite to admission.

Q: Will I learn anything?

A: In order to earn your degree in one year, you're going to receive credit for what you've already learned by passing examinations, by assessment of your life experience, and by learning new material. Contrast earning your degree in one year with the students who take one course a semester over a period of ten years to earn sixty credits. Taking one course a semester is a nuisance, not a commitment. It provides little opportunity for students to integrate their learning from one course to another. Earning your degree in one year requires a commitment on your part—a commitment to learning.

Q: How much does it cost?

A: The cost of earning your degree will depend on the college or university you select, how many credits you need to earn your degree, and how you earn those credits. The cost of examination credits, life experience credits, and course credits are all different. One thing is certain, earning your degree in one year will cost a great deal less than earning your degree over an extended period of time through traditional methods. However, these costs, though reduced, will be compressed into the time frame of a single year and will require a considerable financial commitment on your part.

Q: Can I work full-time and still earn my degree in one year?

A: Of course. If you carefully and wisely choose which college you attend, and if you follow the **One Year to a College Degree Program** conscientiously, it's still possible to earn your degree in one year. In some ways you have an advantage over non-working students since, by using the cooperative education or independent study programs, you can earn credit while at work.

Q: Will I have time for anything else?

A: How you manage your time will be critical in determining how quickly you earn your degree. During the year you will have almost no "free" time. By planning all your time, both the big chunks and the few minutes here and there, you will have time for other activities. You will be able to combine your responsibilities as a full time worker, student, and family member provided you organize and plan time wisely and live by your plan. The free time you previously had available to do nothing or to spend leisurely, you will now have to spend wisely. Trading a year's social and leisure time for a degree that you can use for the rest of your life is a wise bargain.

Q: Is the program only for *A* students or geniuses?

A: The principle behind earning your degree in one year is motivation, not intelligence. If you're smart enough to earn a college degree, you're smart enough to earn it at an accelerated rate.

Resources

An Overview of How It Can Be Done

Bear, John Bjorn *The Alternative Guide to College Degrees and Nontraditional Higher Education*. New York: Stonesong Press, 1980.

Alternative Guide to College Degrees gives adult students information on the different options available for earning a degree besides the traditional on-campus classroom earned degree.

Bear, J. *Bear's Guide to Non-Traditional College Degrees*. Berkeley, CA: Ten Speed Press, 1985.

> *Bear's Guide to Non-Traditional College Degrees* describes numerous approaches to earning a degree without ever taking a single traditional course including Credit for Life Experience, On-the-Job Training, Military Training, and Bible Study; Equivalency Exams; Intensive Study; and, Degree Mills. *Bear's Guide* describes hundreds of innovative programs at colleges and universities that offer fully accredited degrees. It contains an alphabetical directory of schools with data on curriculum, accreditation, degree programs, and student body.

Blaze, Wayne and Nero, John *College Degrees for Adults*. Boston: Beacon Press, 1979.

> *College Degrees for Adults* contains detailed descriptions of 120 college and university programs that offer short residency or non-residency degrees. It offers answers to key questions facing adults considering further education. The programs described are non-traditional, new degree programs, which allow maximum opportunity for self-directed learning. *College Degrees for Adults* is a particularly valuable resource for adults interested in exploring non-traditional alternatives and raises issues that must be confronted by anyone who is planning to enter or re-enter the world of formal education.

Haponski, William C. and McCabe, Charles E. *New Horizons: The Education and Career Guide for Adults*. Princeton, NJ: Peterson's Guides, 1985.

> *New Horizons* covers a broad spectrum of options for adults who want to continue their education, including bachelor's degree, external degree, professional certificate programs, and correspondence courses.

Originally published as *Back to School: The College Guide for Adults*, this new edition places heavier emphasis on career-related aspects of adult education.

Sullivan, Eugene, ed.,*Guide to External Degree Programs in the United States*. 2nd Ed. New York: Collier Macmillan Publishers, 1983.

The second edition of the *Guide to External Degree Programs in the United States* includes new undergraduate and graduate programs as well as updated revisions of those published in the first edition. These programs are designed to meet the needs of working students and other part-time students, who, because of time, financial or other limitations cannot complete a degree program when on-campus classes are required. Off-campus instructional methods described range from independent study projects, correspondence courses to computer-assisted learning and telecommunications technology. These methods have proven to be as effective as regular classroom teaching and are academically sound.

CHAPTER 4
YOU LEARN SOMETHING
NEW EVERY DAY

Most colleges will award credit for education gained through employment, volunteer experiences, political activity, and leisure activities. Through life experience credit, adults who thought their degree was years away can earn up to a year's college credit for experience and knowledge gained five, ten, or even twenty years ago. Schools that give credits based on knowledge gained through life experience recognize that adult learners, students aged twenty-five and older, come to school with a vast background of knowledge that an eighteen- to twenty-two year old college student doesn't have. Through a sophisticated method of assessment, adult learners are awarded credit for their non-school learning experience.

Although these programs are sometimes called "Life Experience Programs," this is a misnomer. The programs don't give you credit for what you have experienced, but rather give credits for what you know. The secret of the successful use of such a program is to match past life experience with current college courses and to prove what you've learned as well as what you've done.

Although there is no exact count of the number of colleges and universities offering credit for life experience, the number of schools with a program to give credit for learning from life experiential learning is growing. Each institution organizes its experiential learning program differently. Although these programs share a common goal to award college credit for past experience, they differ in how many credits are awarded, how they are awarded, and what subjects are eligible for life experience credits.

This chapter describes how you can earn up to thirty college credits by documenting what you've done and what you know. It will help you brainstorm potential areas where you can earn credits, decide how many credits you deserve, and explains how to document your learning.

How Credit is Awarded

Three different models are used to determine how many credits you will be awarded for your post high-school experiences. All three models compare your experiences and knowledge to college level experiences and knowledge. However, they each require you to organize your knowledge differently.

1. **The College Course Model**—The most popular assessment model, the College Course Model, compares a student's life experience to specific college courses. The college course model uses the course descriptions in the course catalog and the more extensive descriptions in the course syllabus to award credit. In order to earn credit for developing black and white photographs in your basement, you must show the knowledge you've gained is equivalent to a college level course in black and white photography.

2. **The Learning Components Model**—The Learning Components Assessment Model allows students to cluster their knowledge in a specific discipline and does not require them to tie it to a specific course. This method is preferred by some colleges because the knowledge you have gained may not match the specific courses the college teaches. You may have learned half of what is taught in one computer course and half of another computer course. The learning components model gives you the advantage of structuring your knowledge and skills the way you learned it rather than the way the college offers it.

3. **The Block Credit Model**—The Block Credits Model allows students to consider their college level learning in light of the depth and breadth of the knowledge obtained by someone who has graduated from college and is

employed in a particular field. When this model is used, you compare your knowledge to the knowledge of someone working in the subject field. The block credit model focuses heavily on employment experiences.

What You Can Earn Credit for

There is an endless array of activities and experiences for which you can earn credit. Don't think you don't know anything. Ask yourself: "What have I done since I graduated from high school; what have I learned from what I have done; where did I learn it?"

Here are some basic areas of your life to consider:

Job Experience. Job experience will probably be your major source of life experience credit. Many of the skills you have earned at work are also taught in college. To determine what you can earn credit for, follow these three steps:

1. List all the jobs you have held.
2. List the duties and responsibilities of each job.
3. List the skills you gained at each job.

Here are typical job skills for which you may be able to earn credit:

- Typing
- Shorthand
- Accounting
- Business Management
- Personnel Management
- Government
- Computer Skills
- Lesson Planning

Volunteer Experience. Many volunteer positions require the skill and have the responsibility of a highly paid professional position. Extensive training is often required before the onset of the volunteer period, and new skills are gained throughout the volunteer process. This training and experience could be eligible for college credit. Here are a few of the many volunteer activities for which you could receive college credit.

- Working for a political candidate or at party headquarters.

- Counseling on a telephone hotline
- Serving as a museum guide
- Working at a homeless shelter
- Performing in a play; working backstage at a play
- Working at a day care center or nursery school
- Coaching a sports team
- Working in a nursing home
- Assisting your child's classroom teacher

Travel Experience. Travel itself is not a creditable experience, but extensive travel experience can often translate into college credit in the areas of foreign language, history, art and architecture. Here are travel related activities that can qualify for credit.

- Living in another country
- Participating in a study tour
- Speaking a foreign language
- Learning the history or culture of a foreign country/people
- Studying the architecture of a country/region
- Studying the wildlife of a region of the world

Adult Education. Adult Education courses are popular. Churches, recreation departments, and private groups all offer adult education courses. Although college credit is traditionally not offered for these courses, these courses may be translated into college credits via life experience.

- Scuba diving
- Parenting education classes
- Flying lessons
- Bible classes
- Real estate classes
- Cardio-Pulmonary Resuscitation (CPR)
- Conversational French, Spanish, or any other language
- Tennis lessons
- Yoga

Leisure Activities. Many Americans devote an extensive amount of time to leisure activities. Of the 168 hours in a week, the average American spends 50 working and commuting to work. Many of the remaining 118 hours are spent

enjoying leisure activities that may be worth college credit.
Here are just a few ideas:

- Playing a musical instrument
- Reading extensively in a particular subject
- Playing on a sports team
- Attending stage plays
- Studying the Bible
- Sailing a boat

List Your Experiences

Here is your chance to brainstorm your life experiences
for which you may be eligible to receive credit.

Employment Experiences

Job 1:_____

Duties:_____

_____

_____

_____

Skills: _____

_____

_____

_____

_____

Job 2: _____

Duties:_____

_____

_____

_____

Skills:_____

_____

_____

_____

_____

Job 3: _____

Duties: _____

_____

_____

_____

Skills: _____

_____

_____

_____

_____

Volunteer Experiences:

Position: _____

Duties: _____

_____

_____

_____

Skills: _____

_____

_____

_____

_____

Position: _____

Duties: _____

_____

_____

_____

Skills: _____

_____

_____

_____

_____

Travel Experiences

Trip: _____

Country/Culture/Language/History/Architecture: _____

_____

_____

Adult Education

Course/Certificate/License/Class: _____
Skills: _____

_____

_____

_____

Course/Certificate/License/Class: _____
Skills: _____

_____

_____

_____

Leisure Activities

Sport/Activity/Past-time: _____
Skills: _____

_____

_____

_____

Sport/Activity/Past-time: _____
Skills: _____

_____

_____

_____

Organizing Your Experience

Once you've listed your experiences, organize your experiences by subject matter. Looking through the college course catalog will help you organize your experiences and assess what you know. You might find it helpful to look through more than one college catalog in order to get different ideas. Using college catalogs could also give you an idea of other experiences that you've had that are creditable. What you earn credit for will vary from college to college depending upon what courses the college offers. For example, Eileen, a licensed private pilot, was not able to earn credit for her pilot's license because the college she attended didn't have a flight school. In retrospect it might have been prudent for her to transfer to a school that did have a flight school since a pilot's license alone might have been worth thirty college credits.

Business. Courses in this area generally include accounting, administration, marketing, real estate, business management, and production management. Activities that may translate into credit include:

- Managing the budget for an organization or office
- Selling or managing real estate
- Doing work related to procurement, billing, or collections
- Operating or managing a business
- Wholesale or retail sales

Computer Science. Computer science departments teach a variety of computer classes that focus both on the use of existing software as well as the design of new software. Activities that could translate into credit in computer science include:

- Using a variety of computer software at work
- Learning to use a personal computer at home
- Writing a computer program
- Learning a computer language
- Taking a non-credit computer class

English and Humanities. Courses in this area generally include philosophy, literature, journalism, writing, and theater. Activities that you could describe in terms of knowledge gained include:

- Reading extensively in a particular area
- Attending a number of plays

- Writing articles for publication
- Work as a writer-editor
- Audio-video production

Foreign Language. Courses in this area typically result in conversational, reading, and writing ability in the Romance, Germanic, Asian, and Mediterranean languages. Ability may have been acquired by doing various jobs.

- Working with people who speak an other language
- Written or oral translator for non-English speaking people
- Living with people who speak a language other than English
- Extended travel to non-English speaking countries
- Self-taught foreign language courses

History. Courses include U.S., European, Middle Eastern, and African history; anthropology, archeology, geography, government, criminology, and political science. There are a great many things you could have done to earn history credits including:

- Reading the newspaper or weekly news magazines
- Keeping a diary or journal of historical events
- Working for local, city, state, or federal government
- Working in a law enforcement organization
- Working for a political campaign
- Working as a newspaper reporter

Music and Art. Courses in music include music appreciation, theater, music history, choral directing, composition, conducting, theory. Courses in art include graphic art, commercial art, drawing, painting, sculpture, and art appreciation. Here are only a few of the many activities that could be a basis for experiential learning in music and art.

- Playing a musical instrument
- Singing in a group
- Dancing
- Drawing, painting
- Sculpting
- Making pottery
- Glass blowing
- Photography

- Creating clothing
- Therapy through art

Social Science. Courses in Social Science include sociology, psychology, and education. You may have learned social science by doing things like:

- Counseling on a telephone hotline
- Volunteering as a teacher's aid
- Working in survey research

Physical Education. Courses in this area generally include health, fitness, and sports instruction. You might be able to describe the knowledge and skill you've gained through a variety of athletic activities to earn course credit. You may be able to earn college credit for:

- Playing a recreational sport
- Extensive experience bicycling, jogging, golfing, playing tennis, or skiing
- Attending aerobics classes
- Certification as a scuba diver or water safety instructor
- Coaching a youth or adult sports team

Science. Generally, science courses are classes in astronomy, biology, chemistry, physics, geology, biochemistry, and botany. Experiences that would generally transfer to college credit include:

- Working at a biology laboratory
- Working as a nurses' aide
- Working at a horticulture laboratory
- Working at a zoo
- Working at a museum

Agriculture. Courses in Agriculture include marketing agricultural products, real property appraisal, product economics, market analysis, agricultural economics, principles of horticulture, and agricultural business economics. You might be able to get credit for a variety of agriculturally related work including:

- Working on a farm
- Working in a farm market
- Working in another agricultural business

Horticulture. Courses or specialties in this area include agronomy, plant pathology, plant physiology, environmental law, floriculture, nursery management, plant production, horticultural therapy, landscape architecture, landscape design, fruit and vegetable production, plant propagation, and tissue culture. Time spent doing one of the following may be turned in to credit.

- Working for an interior plant decorating company
- Working in a florist shop
- Working on a turf farm
- Starting, maintaining or repairing your own lawn
- Doing outdoor landscaping
- Developing landscape designs
- Working in a plant nursery
- Working in an agricultural laboratory

Guidelines for Documenting Your Life Experience

In order to gain credit for what you know, you will have to be able to document what you've learned. Colleges are not just going to give you credit because you say you know something. You have to find ways to prove it.

How to organize your assessment package depends on the college you are attending. Each college sets its own guidelines, but in general a proposal will include two main parts, **a personal narrative** and **course documentation.** The personal narrative is a mini-autobiography; in it you describe yourself and what you've done. The course documentation section lists the courses or learning components for which you are requesting credit and provides justification and supporting documentation for each course.

Usually this information is assembled in a life experience portfolio. Each school sets its own standards for the form and content of the portfolio, but there are some general guidelines for assembling the portfolio and more specific guidelines for its organization into two major sections for the personal narrative and the course list with documentation.

General Guidelines:

1. Package your portfolio for a professional presentation. The neatness, organization, and professional quality of your portfolio tells the reviewing faculty something about you. The quality of your presentation can help to earn you extra credit.

2. Print your written presentation on a quality letter or laser printer. Avoid dot matrix printers. Print your presentation on high quality paper. Make sure your portfolio is completely free of typing, spelling, grammatical, and computer edit errors.

The Personal Narrative:

1. Organize and write your material so that it is easy for the reviewer to read and to understand. Organization and writing clarity are central to success. Write several drafts of your narrative and ask a friend to proof read it. Make sure your narrative is typed and free from errors. Don't rely on "spell check" alone.

2. Be specific. Present details to substantiate your acquired knowledge. Statements like, "I worked in props at a theater for three years," lack essential detail and don't tell what you learned by working in props.

3. Write in a positive and confident manner. Describe your experiences directly. Be sure to stay away from words and expressions that communicate self-doubt and uncertainty. Expressions like "I think," "I might have," "I probably learned," or "approximately" leave the reviewers in doubt.

4. Remember, it's not what you have done, but what you have learned that qualifies for credit. Presenting a litany of experience alone will not earn you college credit. You need to present both what you have done and what you have learned from each experience, logically and coherently.

Courses and Documentation

1. Organize your learning around academic disciplines and specific coursework. Don't expect the reviewer to do your work. Organize your material so the reviewer can eas-

ily relate the description of what you learned to what is taught in a classroom.

2. Show that your learning included specific knowledge, conceptual understanding, and ability to apply the knowledge to your experiences. Colleges expect learning at a minimum of three levels: knowledge, understanding, and application. Show what you know. Show that you understand the material on more than a superficial level. Finally show that you can apply it to a new situation.

3. Show that you understand the theory that underlies your practical knowledge. For example, if you are frequently called on to give speeches, show that you understand the principles of good speech writing and the theory of good speech composition.

4. Verify that you have actually done and learned what you present in your portfolio. Anyone can claim anything. Part of the process of gaining credits for life experience is proving that you have done it. There are two types of documentation: direct and indirect.

Direct documentation are *things you have produced* that prove you have attained a certain level of competency. Typical forms of written documentation include poems, plays, stories, computer programs, manuals, brochures, or books you have written. You can also show examples of artistic or musical talents. Artistic documentation may take the form of photographs, audio and videotapes of performances, recital programs, blueprints, composed music, paintings, sculptures, drawings, or crafts.

In indirect documentation, *other people testify* that you have reached a certain level of competency or have spent a certain number of hours doing a specific task. Usually indirect documentation takes the form of letters written by employers, business partners, consultants, teachers, or volunteer coordinators. Other forms of documentation include commendations, certificates, examples of advertising, receipts from sales, newspaper articles about your work, licenses, military records, course outlines, programs, office job descriptions, and copies of examinations you took.

If you do not have either direct or indirect documentation, you may still be able to earn credit for what you know. Some colleges will allow you to document your knowledge via an oral examination in which a faculty member certifies your level of expertise. Another option is to earn credit via a standardized examination, such as CLEP or ACT. (See chapter 5.)

If there isn't a CLEP or ACT test in your subject area, you still may be able to earn credit in a subject by requesting to challenge a specific course. When you challenge a course, you are given an examination that covers the major content of the course. Not all schools have course challenge opportunities, but many do. (See chapter 8 for more about challenging courses.)

Determining the Number of Credits You Should Request

There are two ways to determine the amount of credit you should request. The first is to match what you know to courses in the course catalog. If your level of Spanish is equal to three semesters of college Conversational Spanish, then you would request nine credits. If you have mastered the techniques taught in Introductory Drawing, you would request three credits.

If there is no course in the catalog that matches what you know, you can use Carnegie units to determine how much credit to request. A Carnegie unit is the method colleges use to determine how much credit to award a particular class. Generally for three college credits, students spend three hours a week in class and spend six hours on work outside of class. During a fifteen-week semester, that amounts to forty-five hours of class time and ninety hours of study time for a total of 135 hours invested to earn three semester hours of credit. Each college credit is worth forty-five hours of study; that's forty-five hours of new learning, not forty-five hours of repeating the same talk over and over.

Because you request a certain number of credits doesn't necessarily mean that the college will award them. The evaluators of your portfolio may judge that your described knowledge, understanding, and application is insufficient to warrant college credit, or your experiential learning deserves some credit but does not represent a full semester's coursework, so the number of credits will be reduced.

Now that you know the basics of experiential learning, here are the answers to some frequently asked questions.

Q. 1: Is there a limit on the number of credits I can earn through experiential learning?

A: Each school is different. Every college has the authority to determine whether or not to award credit for experiential learning, as well as the maximum number of credits to award. The majority of colleges will award a maximum of thirty credits of life experience credit although there are some schools that award more.

Q. 2:   Can the credits earned from experiential learning be applied to any part of my degree program or only to my electives?

A: Again, each school is different. The college has the authority to limit how and when students can use experiential learning credits. Some colleges allow students to use experiential learning credits in any part of their program, while others restrict the application of experiential credits to electives or to any part of the program except their major. Some schools award experiential learning credits in both upper and lower level credits. Some schools will grant experiential credit only in lower level courses.

Q. 3: Can I transfer credits earned through experiential learning?

A: If a school has an experiential learning program, it will normally accept experiential credits awarded by another college or university. The receiving college may reserve the right to redesignate the application of the transferred credits to match its policy regarding use of experiential credits.

Q. 4: Will the credits I earn from experiential learning be immediately applied to my degree, or must I complete a certain number of courses first?

A: The experiential learning credits are applied to your transcript as soon as they are awarded and recording fees, if required, are paid.

Q. 5: What is the cost?

A: The cost of credits earned from life experience varies from college to college, but it is generally much less than the cost of credits earned by traditional college classwork. At certain schools, tuition costs are applied when the credits are awarded. At other schools, tuition is assessed in two stages, an appraisal fee and an award fee. The appraisal fee is charged for having a faculty member evaluate your portfolio. If an appraisal fee is charged, you have to pay this whether or not credits are awarded. Once credits are awarded, a second fee may be charged for posting credits to your transcript.

Q. 6: Do I have to apply for admission to an experiential learning program?

A: Most programs that award credit for prior experiential learning require students to apply for admission to the program. During the application process students briefly explain what courses they would like to earn credit for and why they think they deserve credit. The application process is meant to deter students from entering the program who are unlikely to receive credit.

Q. 7: How are the credit assessments made?

A: The method of credit assessment varies from college to college. In some colleges, even when there is a system, there is often no consensus among the faculty on how to handle individual cases. In a Washington-based university, a student who had written theatrical plays that were produced, applied for life experience credit. The committee disagreed on whether or not to award credit. One group argued that since the university did not offer credit in play writing, credit could not be awarded. Others argued that a college level of competency was achieved and proven and credit should be awarded in English. Individual schools as well as individual faculty members interpret life experience credit in many different ways. Some are very lenient in their interpretation of credit awards and others are very rigid.

Q. 8: Who makes the credit assessment?

A: In general, your portfolio goes to the head of each department from which you requested credit. The department head may delegate the review and evaluation of your portfolio to a department faculty member or may personally review and evaluate your documentation. The department head, however, has responsibility for recommending the award of credits.

Q. 9: Is the best time to begin the assessment process before or after my first semester at the college?

A:If the credits earned through experiential learning may be applied to satisfy degree requirements and not just electives, it would be wise to begin the assessment process before your first semester back in college. This way, you would avoid registering for a course you could more easily earn credit for through experiential learning. If your college will only apply experiential learning credits to electives, it's irrelevant whether you begin the assessment before or after your first semester back at college.

Getting Started

To help you get started organizing potential experiential learning credits, write down the things you have done since high school, the jobs you have held, and the volunteer activities you have participated in. Think of things you have done in your recreation time, your spare time, and your paid time. Think of things you have been taught through on-the-job training, on-the-job observation of the operations of the organization, and any classes or seminars you might have taken. In the **Course** column, write down the title of the courses that may possibly relate to your **Experience** column. Check the course catalog to find as many related courses as possible. Your portfolio will be assessed for credit by each department with a related course so the more related courses, the greater your chance to earn the maximum number of credits.

Now list all the direct and indirect documentation you have or would be able to obtain to prove your knowledge. List your documentation course by course in the **Documentation** column.

As you write your narrative of knowledge gained

through experience, you will need to relate it to the material covered in the related courses.

EXPERIENCE	COURSE	DOCUMENTATION
_____	_____	_____
_____	_____	_____
_____	_____	_____
_____	_____	_____
_____	_____	_____
_____	_____	_____
_____	_____	_____
_____	_____	_____
_____	_____	_____
_____	_____	_____
_____	_____	_____
_____	_____	_____
_____	_____	_____
_____	_____	_____
_____	_____	_____
_____	_____	_____

Available Assistance

You should actively pursue receiving the maximum credits allowed for your experiential learning. There are a lot of resources available to help you.

Workshops and Courses—Most colleges that offer experiential learning credit, offer courses and workshops to assist students in preparing their portfolio for assessment. Some schools require enrollment in a course or workshop while other schools offer optional participation in such workshops. Many schools award three credits for participation in the preparation workshop itself. Even if a workshop or course is not required for you to participate in an experiential learning program, it would be in your best interest to attend just to have the advantage of the experience as well as the many inside tips and personal assistance the staff will provide.

Counselors—In order to assist you in your application for credit for prior experiential learning, most schools have counselors available to help you. These counselors may be located in the Prior Learning Assessment Office, the Adult Learning Service Office, the Testing and Assessment Office, the Continuing Educational Department, or in the External Degree Program Office.

Resources

Credit for Experiential and Extra-institutional Learning

DeLafayette, Jean M. *How to Convert Your Knowledge and Life Experience into Academic Degrees: How to Obtain Your College Degree Through the Evaluation of Personal and Professional Experiences*, 3d. rev. ed. ACUPAE, 1990.

> *How to Convert Your Knowledge and Life Experience* is a methods and strategies manual. It also lists subjects, activities, experiences, talents, skills, information, training, and non-academic learning to be equated to college credit leading to a degree. It contains the amount of credit you may possibly receive as assessed by accredited universities through evaluation of your portfolio of life experience knowledge.

DeLafayette, Jean M. *How Your Portfolio Can Earn You an Accredited College Degree Without Setting Foot on Campus*, 3d. ed. ACUPAE, 1990.

> This guide offers the techniques, methods, and strategies for converting knowledge and life experience into college credits. It describes how to prepare, document, and submit your portfolio.

Heermann, Barry, et al *Credit for Lifelong Learning*, 2d. ed. Tichenor Pub., 1986.

Susan Simosko,*Earn College Credit for What You Know.* Washington, DC: Acropolis Books, 1985.

Earn College Credit for What You Know is a step-by-step guide to earning college credit for life experience. It provides an in-depth explanation of what you may earn life experience for, how to prepare a portfolio that will help you earn the maximum credits for your acquired knowledge, and how your portfolio will be evaluated. If you are considering earning life experience credits by portfolio assessment, *Earn College Credit for What You Know* is a very useful resource.

CHAPTER 5
CREDIT IN 90 MINUTES

Thousands of students each year earn college credit through Credit by Examination programs. Through Credit by Examination Programs, you can receive college credit for what you know, no matter where you learned it. Knowledge gained during leisure reading, in advanced high-school courses, on the job, or while volunteering, can be transformed into easy college credits. Credit by Examination programs do not ask you to document what you know, get letters of support, or submit a portfolio. A passing score on an exam is proof enough that you have the necessary knowledge to earn college credit. Credit by Examination programs can help you to quickly reach your goal of earning a college degree, earning a promotion, or getting into graduate school.

The advantages of earning credit by examination are numerous. Here are just a few:

1. **Cost savings.** Credit by Examination programs charge a fraction of regular college tuition costs. For example, if a testing program charges $50 to earn three credits by examination and the college or university that you are attending charges $100 a credit or $300 for a three-credit course, the three credits earned by exam would save you $300 less the $50 testing fee, or $250. If the college or university you are attending charges more per credit, and most do, your savings would be even greater. Multiply this savings by several courses, and the overall savings is substantial.

2. **Quick accumulation of credits.** Although most colleges limit the number of CLEP credits a student may take in their degree program, there are no limits on the num-

ber of examinations a student may take in a single semester. Be cautioned, though, that some schools set a limit on the number of CLEP or ACT credits allowed during your final thirty credit hours of registered classes. You could plan to take one or two exams a semester or you could take four exams a month and potentially earn up to sixty credits in a single semester.

3. **Time saving.** Credit by examination offers students an opportunity to earn credit at a tremendous time savings. A three-credit course involves forty-five hours of class time, ninety hours to study and complete class assignments, and travel time based on the number of times the class meets per week and the distance from home to school. Earning credit by examination can save you a tremendous amount of time. Even if you have very little background in the subject and must spend time learning the subject, you will save classroom time and commuting time.

4. **Written Assignments.** When you earn credits by examination, you avoid the aggravation of writing papers. Most college courses require two, three, or four papers of varying length. Papers are time consuming and often require extensive library research. Students also complain that the papers are subjectively graded and the grades reflect the bias of the teacher rather than the quality of the paper. By earning credit through examination, you avoid the subjectivity of grading and the time and effort involved in writing papers.

5. **Bypass introductory level courses.** Most of the courses that are offered by examination are at the introductory level. By taking exams in place of introductory courses, you will be able to satisfy the introductory level course requirements and move quickly to advanced classes that are more exciting and relevant to your interests. Many students complain that core requirements are tedious and unnecessary. By earning credit through examination, you can get core requirements out of the way and take courses in your major sooner.

6. **Improve college admission chances.** Earning credit by examination prior to applying for admission signals

college admissions offices that you are capable of doing college level work. It targets you as a highly motivated student.

The Process

Step One—Get Information

The two major testing programs are the College Level Examination Program administered by the College Board, which is the same organization that administers the SAT and the GRE, and the Proficiency Examination Program administered by the American College Testing Program, the same people who administer the ACT. Contact both of these organizations for information and registration materials. Their addresses are:

> CLEP (College Level Examination Program)
> Educational Testing Service
> Princeton, NJ 08541
> (215) 750-8420

> ACT/PEP (American College Testing Program/
> Proficiency Examination Program)
> P.O. Box 168
> Iowa City, IA 52243
> (319) 337-1419

Step Two—Register for Selected Examinations

You must register for CLEP exams four weeks in advance and ACT/PEP exams six weeks in advance. On the registration form you will be asked to provide your name, address, phone number, what tests you want to take, the location where you want to be tested, and to which school you want your scores sent. You must also send the registration fee with your registration application. You will receive a portion of the registration application back in the mail. It will be your ticket of admission to the test.

Step Three—Take the Exam

Be sure to arrive early at the examination site. Leave enough time to account for heavy traffic, finding your way around the college campus, parking, and finding the right test room. Once the exam has begun, you cannot be admitted. You will need to bring your admission form, an identification with photograph, several No. 2 pencils, a watch, and a black pen if you will be writing essays. Books, notes, dictionaries, or other study materials are not allowed in the testing room. You may be permitted to use a silent calculator if it can be erased of user programs. Take a jacket or sweater with you to the testing site since you might need it to stay comfortable.

Step Four—Scoring

The time it takes to score the exams depends on who is administering the exam. CLEP generally takes three to four weeks to score their exams, while PEP takes four to five weeks for scoring exams. If the exam has an essay portion, you must wait for your individual college to score the essay. This could take from two to four weeks additional time. Although testing agencies provide colleges and universities with recommended passing scores, each college sets its own passing score and determines the number of credits awarded. Consequently, a passing score on the same exam may be worth three credits at one college, but six or nine credits at another school. Scores are reported in standard scores and percentile rank. Your percentile rank will tell you what percentage of the students taking the test scored at or below your score.

Posting. Over twenty-five hundred colleges and universities around the world recognize credit by examination programs and are willing to award credit for a passing score on an exam. It is important to know that scores or grades are not posted on your transcript, only the title of the course examination and the credits awarded. If you should fail to receive a passing score on an exam, the fact that you attempted the examination and failed it is not posted on your transcript.

In-depth Description of the Programs
The College Level Examination Program (CLEP)

The College Level Examination Program has been in existence since 1968. CLEP is the most widely accepted Credit by Examination program in the country. CLEP examinations cover material that is taught in introductory level courses at most colleges and universities. CLEP examinations are offered by the College Board, a non-profit organization that provides tests for students, schools, and colleges. Offered on a monthly basis, CLEP examinations are administered at more than twelve hundred locations across the country during different days of the same week each month.

There are a total of thirty-eight CLEP examinations. Of these, five are classified as General Examinations and thirty-three are classified as Subject Examinations. The General Examinations cover the broad material usually studied during the first two years of a four-year college curriculum. The Subject Examinations cover courses usually taught as single college courses.

Over three-fourths of all accredited colleges and universities give credit for CLEP. However, be careful. Just because a college is listed as one that awards credit for CLEP examinations doesn't mean it will award credit for every CLEP examination. Some colleges will award credit for the Subject Examinations, but not for the General Examinations. While for other colleges, the reverse is true. Other colleges leave it up to each individual department to decide whether CLEP credits will be accepted.

The cost of CLEP examinations is minimal. In 1991 each examination cost thirty-eight dollars regardless of the number of credits awarded. Current prices are available through the CLEP office. Active military personnel may take CLEP examinations without charge through the DANTES Program. (Defense Activity for Traditional Educational Support.)

The CLEP General Examinations uses the same scale as the SAT. That is, you will receive a score from two hun-

dred to eight hundred. Subject examination scores range from
twenty to eighty. The multiple choice section of the examinations is scored by machine. Except for the English Composition Essay exam, all essays are evaluated and graded only
by the colleges that require them and are not scored or graded
by CLEP. The colleges and universities decide how to weight
the multiple choice and essay portions of each exam and
whether or not to award a passing score.

The General Examinations

The College Board offers five General CLEP examinations of material covered in courses taken during the first
two years of college. Each is ninety minutes long and composed entirely of multiple choice questions, except for the
English Composition Examination with Essay. The five
General Examinations are:

English Composition—This examination tests the
student's ability to write in standard written English and tests
the student's ability to explain, interpret, analyze, and
support a given viewpoint. There are two versions of this
examination, one made entirely of multiple choice questions
and the other containing forty-five minutes of multiple choice
and forty-five minutes of essay questions. The English Composition Examination with Essay is graded by two professors employed by CLEP. The points that each professor
awards are added to the score of the multiple choice examination.

Humanities—The subjects covered by the examinations include Literature, Drama, Poetry, Music and Art.

Mathematics—The topics covered in the examinations
include Algebra, Geometry, Probability and Statistics, Logic
and Sets, Functions, and the Real Number System.

Natural Sciences—The topics covered in the examinations include General Biology, Physical Science,
Geology, and Astronomy.

Social Sciences and History—The examination top-
ics include Political Science, Economics, Sociology,
Psychology, U.S. History, Western Civilization, African and
Asian Civilizations.

The Subject Examinations

The Subject Examinations are more specific than the General Examinations and usually include material covered in a single college level course. Subject Examinations are also multiple choice and ninety minutes long. Most Subject Examinations also have an essay section that is to be taken only if it is required by your college.

Here is a list of CLEP Subject Examinations:

HISTORY AND SOCIAL SCIENCES
American Government
American History I
American History II
Western Civilization I
Western Civilization II
General Psychology
Educational Psychology
Human Growth and Development
Introductory Sociology
Introductory Microeconomics
Introductory Macroeconomics

FOREIGN LANGUAGES
College French—Levels 1 & 2
College German—Levels 1 & 2
College Spanish—Levels 1 & 2

COMPOSITION AND LITERATURE
American Literature
Analysis and Interpretation of Literature
College Composition
English Literature
Freshman English

SCIENCE AND MATHEMATICS
Calculus with Elementary Functions
College Algebra
Trigonometry
College Algebra-Trigonometry
General Biology
General Chemistry

BUSINESS
Computers and Data Processing
Introduction to Management
Introductory Accounting
Introductory Business Law
Introductory Marketing

Resources—If you decide to take one or more CLEP Examinations, there are several resources available to help you. *The College Board Guide to CLEP Examinations* (The College Board, New York, 1987) offers a complete description of all the exams, an outline of the topics contained on the exams, along with the percentages of the exam that cover each topic, a list of study resources, and twenty-five sample questions.

The ACT/PEP

The Proficiency Examination Program (PEP) uses the examinations given for more than a decade by the University of the State of New York Regents College Degrees. Since 1963 the colleges and universities in New York and other states have awarded credits based on these examinations. The PEP Examinations are intended to test college level proficiency in arts and sciences, business, education, and nursing. The examinations test not only how well you know facts and terminology, but how well you can apply this information. Tests are developed by a committee of college professors who have taught the subject being tested, in conjunction with test specialists to assure that the test accurately measures what it purports to measure.

The PEP Exams are offered six times a year by the American College Testing Program at over one hundred locations around the country. However, not all centers test on each test date, and not all exams are offered on all test dates. Scores on the PEP exams range from twenty (low) to eighty (high). Most of the ACT/PEP exams are three hours long. Several of the business essays are four hours long and the examination for Reading Instruction: Application is six hours long. You may take up to four exams on each test date.

Study guides for each exam are available free of charge

by writing, ACT/PEP, P.O. Box 168, Iowa City, IA 52243
(319) 337-1419.

Here is a list of ACT/PEP Examinations:

ARTS AND SCIENCES
Abnormal Psychology
Anatomy and Physiology
Foundations of Gerontology
Microbiology
Physical Geology
Statistics

BUSINESS
Corporation Finance
Introductory Accounting
Principles of Management
Principles of Marketing
Production/Operations Management

EDUCATION
Educational Psychology
Reading Instruction in the Elementary School
Reading Instruction: Theoretical Foundations

NURSING
Fundamentals of Nursing
Maternity Nursing
Maternal and Child Nursing I & II
Adult Nursing
Psychiatric/Mental Health Nursing
Commonalities in Nursing Care I & II
Differences in Nursing Care I & II
Occupational Strategies in Nursing
Professional Strategies in Nursing
Health Support I & II

Challenging a College Course

The third way to earn college credit by examination is
to challenge a college course. If the college or university
you are attending doesn't give credit for CLEP or ACT/PEP
exams, or if they do give credit, but they don't offer an ex-

amination in a subject area that you have knowledge in, you can request to challenge a college course by taking an examination prepared by the department.

Challenging a college course is similar to taking a CLEP or ACT/PEP exam. You can receive credit for what you know without having to go to class, write papers, or complete assignments. But there are differences that could make challenging a college course more difficult than taking a CLEP or ACT/PEP exam. The format of the exam will vary from department to department, exam to exam, and school to school. Professors may elect to give a multiple choice, true/false, short answer, and/or essay question exams. The exam may even require an oral test in addition to a written section.

The cost of challenging a college exam varies from school to school. Some schools have a standard fee, but most charge full tuition based on a per credit charge. So, even though there may be little or no cost savings when challenging an exam, the time and energy savings alone should make it worth your while.

If you are interested in challenging an exam, check with the college or university you plan to attend, or are currently enrolled, to find out the policy regarding challenging courses.

Selecting Exams

Selecting the correct exams to take is a critical step in your success toward earning credit by examination.

Guidelines

Before you select an exam, find out as much as possible about the content of each exam. You will need to get information about which exams are lower level course exams and which are upper level since lower level exams should be taken before upper level ones.

Read the test description provided for each exam in the test materials. Get a copy of the syllabus. Look through textbooks in that subject. Get books such as *The College Board Guide to CLEP* which has twenty-five sample questions for each of the General and Subject Examinations.

1. Pick exams that you have a strong background in. By selecting exams that cover information you already know, you can pass proficiency exams with little or no effort. Knowledge you gained in a high-school course, military course, television course, a non-credit course, college course you dropped or failed, on-the-job training, through volunteer work, or while reading, could all help you to pass a proficiency examination. Here are just a few examples; the possibilities are endless:

If you have a good high-school math background, you could probably pass College Algebra, Trigonometry, or College Algebra with Trigonometry. With a strong science background, you might also be able to pass General Biology and General Chemistry.

If you are a native speaker or learned, conversational speaker of French, German, or Spanish, you could easily pass Levels I & II of these exams.

If you work with computers on a regular basis, you could probably pass Information Systems and Computer Applications.

If you took General Psychology in college, without much study effort you should be able to pass Human Growth and Development, Abnormal Psychology, and Introduction to Educational Psychology.

If you took courses, workshops, or seminars at work that covered the basic principles of Marketing, Accounting, or Management, you should be able to use this knowledge to gain credit in these areas.

2. Sign up for exams that overlap. Don't think of the CLEP and the ACT/PEP exams as distinct exams but rather as clusters of exams. Often the exams overlap so you can reduce your study time dramatically by focusing on exams that do overlap rather than those that test distinct pools of information.

For example, General Psychology, Human Growth and Development, and Introduction to Educational Psychology form an exam cluster. General Psychology and Educational Psychology have large areas of overlap. Both cover perception, research methods, statistics, cognition, and development. Educational Psychology applies the material contained in General Psychology to a classroom setting. Both Educational Psychology and General Psychology have large Human Development components. When you've studied for either of these exams, you've also studied for the Human Growth and Development exam as well. The best advice is that if you sign up for one of these three exams, sign up for all three. Sign up for the lower level exams first, then the upper level.

Examples of other exams that overlap include Reading Instruction in the Elementary School (ACT/PEP) and Reading Instruction: Theoretical Foundations (ACT/PEP), General Biology (CLEP) and Anatomy and Physiology (ACT/PEP), English Composition (CLEP) and Freshman English (CLEP), American Government (CLEP) and American History (CLEP).

3. Take examinations for lower level courses before taking upper level course examinations. CLEP and ACT/PEP do not assign course numbers or levels to the exams, but many colleges do. Match the CLEP and ACT/PEP courses to the corresponding courses in the course catalog of your college. Some colleges do not allow you to earn credit for lower level courses or exams after you have earned upper level credit in the same area. For example, if you first took the exam for Human Growth and Development, an upper level course, you might not be awarded the credit for General Psychology, a lower level course, which you took second.

4. Select more courses than you need. You can't expect to pass every single exam you take. If you need twenty-one examination credits, plan to take examinations worth thirty credits. Don't wind up delaying your degree because you expected to pass a particular exam and didn't. Don't wait until you receive your exam results before registering to take your next exam. If you overbook your exams and find out later that you have enough credits, you can cancel the exam and receive a refund for the exam fee.

5. Pick exams that fit your degree program. Match the exams to the core requirements, major requirements, and minor requirements of your degree program. If you need a Social Science or English course for graduation, take these. If you can pass an exam easily and don't need it to satisfy a degree requirement, use it as an elective.

6. **Pick exams that your college will give you credit for.** Just because a college awards credit for CLEP and ACT/PEP exams doesn't mean it gives credit for every CLEP or ACT/PEP exam. Decisions are often made on a department by department basis. You might need to contact each department individually or find out from a central student service office which examinations are accepted.

Study Strategies

The amount of time required to study for ACT/PEP or CLEP will depend on your previous and current knowledge in a particular area. For some examinations, no preparation will be needed. Other exams could require extensive preparation on your part. Take one step at a time.

1. **Obtain the study guide from ACT/PEP or CLEP for the examination you wish to take.** These study guides are available free of charge and will help you prepare the most efficiently for the exam. The study guide will contain a list of the topics covered on the test as well as the percentage of questions asked about each, sample test questions, and a list of references from which you can study.

2. **Obtain a textbook recommended by the test developer.** You might be able to obtain the textbook you need from a public library. If not, go to a college library or college bookstore. If you can't get the textbook you want, find a textbook that covers the same topics. A recent edition will contain more current information than an older textbook; however, any edition within the past five years will provide adequate information to help you pass an exam. You only need to study one textbook for each exam. Don't confuse yourself with several sources.

Study the outline provided by the test publisher and highlight the areas you do know. Match the areas you don't know to the chapters in the textbooks. Make a list of the chapters you need to study.

3. Once you know what you must study, establish regular study sessions. Preset a time each day and stick to it. You may choose to study on your lunch hour, in the mornings before work, or during the two hours after dinner and before you go to bed. Whatever time you select, stick to it. If you study two hours a day, it should take you one month, or approximately sixty hours to study for a single exam. If you have a strong background in the subject, you will need less time.

Once you decide when you are going to study, decide where to study. Pick a quiet place that is free from distractions. You might choose to go to the library for help. College libraries have quiet areas and individual carrels for students to use. If your home is noisy, a visit to the library should pay off if it is close by.

4. Organize each study session into three parts.

Part One—Overview Get an overview of the material you are about to study by reading the introduction, leafing through the chapter and noting the section headings, and carefully reading the summary. If there are questions at the end of the chapter, read these carefully since they will tell you what the author thinks is important.

Part Two—Intensive Study Now read the chapter. Make questions out of the section headings and answer them as you read. For example, if it says "CAUSES OF THE CIVIL WAR," ask yourself, "What were the causes of the Civil War?" "CELL METABOLISM" could be reformulated as, "What are the stages of cell metabolism?"

As you read, use two pages to take notes. On the top of one sheet of paper, write the word "CONCEPT" and as you read, list the key concepts. Don't try to list or memorize all the details contained in the chapter. On a second page write the word "VOCABULARY" and write all the vocabulary words and their definitions.

Part Three—Review and Self-Testing Review your notes. Reread the chapter summary and outline it. Answer the questions in the back of the chapter. If possible, practice taking a multiple choice test either at the end of the chapter or contained in a study guide that comes with the textbook.

5. The final review is the last step of the preparation process. One week before the testing date, you should have all your reading done and be ready for a final review. Review your notes. You should have four sections of notes for each chapter you read. These four sections—a list of key concepts, a list of vocabulary with definitions, an outline of the chapter summary, and the answers to chapter questions—are the key to your success.

Test Taking Strategies

Doing well on a proficiency exam involves knowing the subject matter and knowing how to take a test. Good test taking strategies are no substitute for knowledge, but they can help you to obtain a score that reflects what you do know.

The format of a CLEP or ACT/PEP exam is a multiple choice exam with a possible essay component. Professional test designers use a multiple choice test for a variety of reasons: they are easy to grade, can cover a lot of subject matter, and are objective. Unknowledgeable test takers often call multiple choice "multiple guess," but that nickname is far from accurate. In reality, multiple choice exams provide the most accurate picture of a student's knowledge.

In order to do well on a multiple choice exam, it is helpful to understand the parts of a multiple choice question and how they work together to form a question that accurately measures what you know. Here is a simple, yet effective multiple choice question.

What is the capital of New York?

      A. Albany   C. Manhattan

      B. Buffalo   D. New York City

A multiple choice question is made up of four parts: a **STEM, ALTERNATIVES, the CORRECT ANSWER, and DISTRACTORS.** The STEM is the part of the question that asks the question. In the sample question, the stem is "What is the capital of New York?" The ALTERNATIVES are the list of choices from which you try to identify the correct answer. The sample question has four answer choices. The CORRECT ANSWER is the answer that the test writer decides is correct. In the sample, the correct an-

swer is *A. Albany*. DISTRACTORS are the wrong answers.
A good distractor is plausible to the uninformed. A good
distractor shouts "Pick me, Pick me, Pick me." When a
multiple choice test is scored, each question is given the same
weight when determining your score. Whether the question
is easy or hard, it is only worth one point.

Four Rules for Multiple Choice Success

1. **Read the question and try to answer it before looking at the given alternatives.** Once you think you know
the answer, look and see if you find your answer among the
alternatives. If the answer is there, select it; don't worry
about any other alternatives. Remember distractors are meant
to entice you. Reading them when you already know the
answer will only confuse you and waste testing time. If your
answer is not there, carefully reread the stem. You probably
misread the question. If it is a math problem, recalculate.

2. **If you don't know the answer, study the alternatives and eliminate the incorrect choices.** Use logic to
eliminate incorrect answers. If two answers overlap or are
opposite, then one must be wrong. Cross out the choices
you're sure are wrong and guess from the remaining choices.
Put a question mark next to the question in your test booklet
so that if you finish the test early, you can come back and
take a second look at it.

3. **If you are confused by a question, study the stem.**
Items are often missed when they are read quickly and care-
lessly. Reread the stem slowly. You might have overlooked
vital clues. Watch out for words such as *never, always, occasionally, sometimes,* and *except*. They can change the
entire meaning of a question. If you're still confused by the
question, skip it and mark it with a double question mark to
come back to if you have time at the end. Don't waste time
on items you have little chance of getting right.

4. **If there is no penalty for guessing, then be sure to
select an answer for every question.** If there is a penalty
for guessing, then only guess if you can eliminate at least
one of the alternatives. CLEP exams do have a penalty for

guessing, so do not guess randomly. If you don't finish the exam, do not fill in the rest of the questions. However, ACT/PEP exams do not have a penalty for guessing, so if you don't have time to finish the exam, make sure all the answer blanks are filled in.

Pacing is essential to success on a timed exam. Bring a watch to check the time and to determine how much time you have left. When half the time is up, you should be finished with half the questions. If not, it's time to speed up.

Here are a few tips that will help you work faster and more efficiently.

1. Position your answer sheet next to your booklet so that you can mark your answers quickly on the answer sheet without moving either the booklet or the answer sheet.

2. Know the directions before you take the exam. This way you will not have to waste valuable exam time reading directions.

3. Get a copy of the answer sheet that will be used during the test and practice using it. Know whether you answer the questions vertically or horizontally on the answer sheet.

4. Take notes and do calculations right on the test booklet. Do not bother with scraps of paper.

5. Be familiar with the format of the exam. Know how many items there are and how long you have to complete them.

6. If you finish early, first check your answer sheet. Make sure you didn't skip any questions or answer any questions twice. If you answered a question twice, all your answers will be out of alignment.

7. After you check your answer sheet and correct any mistakes, go back and retry the questions you skipped or were unsure of. Something on the exam might have given you a clue on how to solve the questions you left unanswered or jar your memory about the missing information.

Anwering Essay Questions

Answering an essay question effectively requires an entirely different set of skills. Essay questions require you to supply the correct answer, rather than just recognize it. Essay questions also require you to organize and integrate large amounts of information rather than remembering specific facts or applying a specific theory.

Start answering any essay question by reading the question twice. Underline key phrases and make notes next to the question that will help you organize your answer. Be

A Penalty for Guessing

Some test manufacturers penalize guessing, while others do not. The standard penalty for guessing is computed by subtracting a certain percentage of the wrong answers from the number of correct answers. Tests with five alternative answers traditionally subtract 1/4 of the wrong answers. Tests with four choices usually subtract 1/3 of the wrong answers.

Example: A student is taking a one hundred-item multiple choice exam with five answer alternatives. The student knows sixty of the one hundred questions, can eliminate some of the choices in twenty questions, and has no idea of the answer in the remaining twenty questions. What is the impact on the student's score for not guessing, selectively guessing, or randomly guessing?

Not guessing:

Number right - Number wrong = 60 - 0 = 60

Selectively guessing:

Number right-1/4 Number wrong. 60 correct, 20 educated guesses, (12 correct and 8 incorrect), and 20 questions omitted.

60 + 12-8/ 4 = 70

Randomly guessing:

60 correct, 20 educated guesses, (12 correct and 8 incorrect) and 20 questions guessed randomly (4 correct and 16 incorrect)..

60 + (12-8/ 4) + (4-16) = 70

The resulting score after all adjustments are made is called a formula score. This score is converted to a standard score from twenty to eighty, or two hundred to eight hundred so that one exam can be compared to another. Formula scores cannot be compared since all the exams have a different number of questions and a different level of difficulty. It is impossible to compare one set of scores to another unless they are standardized.

sure you understand what the question wants. Next, take a minute to organize your thoughts. Outline your answer to the question. Go back and reread the question to make sure the outline matches the question.

Now you are ready to begin writing. Write your answer in good English. Use all the time allotted. Don't write a brief answer in twenty minutes and leave the exam early. On the other hand, don't get so involved in details that you don't have time to finish your answer.

If you have to answer several questions, answer the easiest ones first. Budget your time, don't get stuck on a difficult question and fail to answer the rest of the exam.

Coping With Anxiety

Often adult students fail to return to college because of a fear of tests. Fear of failure produces anxiety at such a tremendous level that it becomes impossible to think clearly.

A positive attitude can help reduce anxiety. Think positively. You can pass the exam. Remember you are not expected to get all the questions right. If you're not sure of an answer, you can always guess through the process of elimination. Being well prepared also reduces anxiety. Study well in advance. Don't try to cram for an exam a few days before. Set a schedule and stick to it. If you find yourself getting scared, don't fret, study more. Taking productive action reduces anxiety because it gives you a sense of control. Worrying increases anxiety because it wastes time and heightens negative thoughts.

Knowing about the test and the testing process will also help reduce your anxiety. Familiarize yourself with the test in advance. Visit the place you will take the test, even have a look inside the classroom. The more you know what to expect, the less frightening taking the exam will be.

The night before the exam, go to bed early and get a good night's rest. Don't take a sedative because it will only make you groggy during the exam the next morning. On the morning of the exam, eat a good breakfast. Don't stuff yourself or you'll feel groggy. Eat enough to carry you through the morning.

Resources
Credit by Examination

American Council on Education *The Guide to Educational Credit by Examination*. New York: Macmillan Publishing Company, 1991.

The Credit by Examination Program of the American Council on Education evaluates examinations and examination programs in terms of educational credit. *The Guide to Educational Credit by Examination*, intended primarily as a reference for colleges and academic advisors, publishes the results of their evaluations, including content and technical review summaries, general subject areas or course equivalents, and gives the Council's recommendations for the amount of credit and minimum score at which a credit award is justified. The *Guide* evaluates the College Level Examination Program (CLEP), the University of the State of New York Regents College Examination Program (RCE; ACT/PEP), Defense Activity for Non-Traditional Educational Support (DANTES) Subject Standardized Tests, test offered by the U.S. Department of State, and the American Chemical Society among others. Credit recommendations have also been established for some licensure and certification examinations, such as the Registered Professional Court Reporter Examination, the Certified Professional Secretary Examination, and the examinations of the National Institute for Automotive Service Excellence. The credit equivalencies in the *Guide* are recommendations; the actual determination of credit awarded is dependent on institutional policy.

Gruber, G.*CLEP (College-Level Examination Program)* New York: Monarch Press, 1983.

CLEP (College-Level Examination Program) is a two-part study guide aimed at helping students earn CLEP credit. Part I contains two practice tests patterned after an actual test. Part II contains a comprehensive math refresher geared toward CLEP General Examination in mathematics. Topics covered include arithmetic, algebra, plane geometry, analytical geometry, and graphs and charts.

Hawes, Gene *Getting College Credits by Examination*. New York: McGraw-Hill.

Getting College Course Credits by Examination describes in detail all the equivalency exams offered by the College Board and the American College Testing Program. It offers suggestions for studying for each test and provides sample questions.

Lieberman, L., Spielberger, J., Erdsneker, B., Heller, R., and Woloch, N. *CLEP (College-Level Examination Program)* 2d ed. New York: Arco Publishing, 1985.

The *College-Level Examination Program* contains fifteen full-length examinations with an explanation for every correct answer. It has three complete practice examinations for each of the five General Examination areas: English Composition, Humanities, Mathematics, Natural Sciences, and Social Science and History. It contains diagnostic charts to help students assess their own strengths and weaknesses in each General Examination area. Besides sample practice tests, *College-Level Examination Program* provides readers with a lot of helpful information including: when and where CLEP tests are given, how to register for the exams, how the CLEP tests are scored, how scores are reported, hints for scoring high, test taking tips, study hints, a description of each General Examination, and a selected biography.

CHAPTER 6
DO YOU HAVE A RECORD?

The quickest, easiest, and cheapest way to earn credits toward your degree is to get credit for classes you've taken, either in a college or in another instructional setting. These credits are already earned and paid for, and if you're going to graduate in one year, it'll be much easier if you use every one you possibly can.

Many students with a previously earned college record choose not to use it even though it would shorten the time it would take them to earn their college degree. Here are a few of the most common reasons students choose not to report previous educational experience.

1. Afraid it will hinder their chances of being admitted to college. Many students fear that if their past academic record were known they would have little chance of getting into the college of their choice. In an attempt to gain enrollment into a competitive college, some students choose to pretend they never went to college and stand on their high-school record alone.

Just because you did poorly in school five, ten, fifteen, or even twenty years ago doesn't mean you're a poor educational risk now. Colleges understand that adult students are more mature and highly motivated than when they initially attended college. Further, most colleges require a full disclosure of past academic performance. They insist on knowing all past educational experiences, and failure to reveal this information would constitute fraud.

2. Embarrassed about their poor record. Many students who dropped out of college did so because of a poor academic record. Ashamed of this past record, they would rather start over than have their new advisor see their past record. But, because college credits are expensive in terms of both time and money, valuable credits hidden inside a dismal record should be applied to a new degree.

3. *Assume the college credits they have will not be accepted.* Many students assume the college credits they have will not be accepted by the college of their choice. Foreign students often think that the credits they earned at home will not be accepted for transfer. Students who attended colleges that were not accredited often fail to present these credits for transfer. Students who took workshops at work or through professional organizations do not know that these courses are sometimes eligible for college transfer.

Classes taken at accredited and non-accredited universities, foreign universities, and in non-university settings should all be applied for transfer. Colleges may disallow the credit you request, but if you don't request these credits, you're certainly not going to be able to count the acceptable transfer credits toward your goal of 120 credits.

Where Can You Find College Degrees?

The number of ways to earn credit in American society is extensive. Public and private institutions provide the primary method of earning college credit. Formal instruction at the post-secondary level is also provided by businesses, government, industry, the military, associations and unions. You may be able to get credit put directly on your transcript for a variety of activities including courses taken at a junior or community college ten, twenty, or even thirty years ago; a computer course taught at your workplace; a scuba diving course taught by the Professional Association of Diving Instructors; flying lessons taught by a certified flight instructor; or a communications course taught in the military.

There are four sources of college credit that can be considered for transfer:

Accredited Colleges and Universities

Non-accredited colleges
Credit from foreign universities
Non-college learning

Each of these four sources will be discussed in depth to help you receive the maximum transfer credits from your past educational experience.

Accredited Colleges and Universities:

In most countries the government charters and administers colleges and universities, assuring certain standards and quality. In the United States, education is under the control of the individual states rather than the federal government. Each state can sets its own educational standards for schools, colleges, and universities under its jurisdiction. Both public and private educational institutions must follow the minimum guidelines imposed by each state but may impose stricter standards as they deem necessary. The diversity of educational institutions within each state is immense, from large state universities to highly competitive private schools, to very small, relaxed private schools.

Without a system of accreditation, transfer of college credit within states and between states would be impossible. Colleges would have no assurances of the instructional quality, course content, or faculty quality. There are over three thousand different colleges in the United States. It's impossible for college admissions officers to know each of these colleges individually, so they rely on various accrediting institutions to assure the quality of colleges and universities. Accrediting bodies make the transfer of credit from one institution to another possible. There are three types of accrediting bodies: regional, national, and professional.

Most admissions officers rely on **regional accrediting commissions,** which accredit traditional colleges and universities within a particular region. There are six regional accrediting bodies responsible for accrediting all colleges and universities in the United States, Guam, Puerto Rico, and the Virgin Islands. If you are interested in finding out whether a particular college is accredited by a regional commission, look in the college catalog. Accredited colleges are proud to publish their accreditation status, e.g., "Accredited by the Middle States Association of Colleges and Schools." If such information is noticeably lacking, call the college admissions office and ask about college accreditation. Unless you are considering attending a professional school or limiting your education to Bible colleges and technical schools, you should get your degree from a college accredited by one of the following six regional accrediting bodies:

1. **Middle States Association of Colleges and Schools**, with its office in Philadelphia, Pennsylvania (215-662-5606), is responsible for granting accreditation to colleges and universities in Delaware, the District of Columbia, Maryland, New Jersey, New York, Pennsylvania, Puerto Rico, and the Virgin Islands.

2. **New England Association of Schools and Colleges**, with its office in Winchester, Massachusetts (617-729-6762), is responsible for granting accreditation to colleges and universities in Connecticut, Maine, Massachusetts, New Hampshire, Rhode Island, and Vermont.

3. **North Central Association of Colleges and Schools**, with its office in Chicago, Illinois (312- 263-0456), is responsible for granting accreditation to colleges and universities in Arizona, Arkansas, Colorado, Illinois, Indiana, Iowa, Kansas, Michigan, Minnesota, Missouri, Nebraska, New Mexico, North Dakota, Ohio, Oklahoma, South Dakota, West Virginia, Wisconsin, and Wyoming.

4. **Northwest Association of Schools and Colleges**, with its office in Seattle, Washington (206-543-0195), is responsible for granting accreditation to colleges and universities in Alaska, Idaho, Montana, Nevada, Oregon, Utah, and Washington.

5. **Southern Association of Colleges and Schools**, with its office in Decatur, Georgia (404-329-6500), is responsible for granting accreditation to colleges and universities in Alabama, Florida, Georgia, Kentucky, Louisiana, Mississippi, North Carolina, South Carolina, Tennessee, Texas, and Virginia.

6. **Western Association of Schools and Colleges**, with its office in Oakland, California (415-688-7575), is respon-

sible for granting accreditation to colleges and universities in California, Guam, and Hawaii.

National accrediting bodies accredit specialized institutions in a particular area. National accrediting bodies include:

- American Association of Bible Colleges
- Association of Advanced Rabbinical and Talmudic Schools
- The Association of Independent Colleges and Schools
- Association of Theological Schools in the U.S. and Canada
- National Association of Trade and Technical Schools
- The National Home Study Council

Professional organizations accredit free-standing professional schools and professional programs within multi-purpose institutions. For example, the American Psychological Association accredits doctoral programs in psychology; the American Association for Counseling and Development accredits master's and doctoral level programs in counseling; and the American Library Association accredits programs in librarianship.

The whole issue of accreditation can get quite complicated. In fact, institutions may have several types of accreditation. For example, doctoral programs in psychology are located in departments or schools that are housed in colleges and universities. The specific program may be accredited by the American Psychological Association (APA), and the college may be accredited by a regional accrediting body. The same college may have a School of Business that may or may not be accredited by the American Assembly of Collegiate Schools of Business.

With so many types of accreditation available, it's difficult to know which is the most important. In terms of transfer credit, regional accreditation is the most important. It's difficult, although not impossible, to transfer credits from one school to another if they are not from a regionally accredited college or university. In terms of securing a job or securing professional certification, professional accreditation is crucial. When you apply for a job, most employers don't ask if the college you attended was accredited by a regional accrediting body—although in many professions, graduating from an accredited program is a prerequisite to obtaining a license to practice. For example, if you want to transfer from one psychology program to another, your original school's regional accreditation is most crucial. If you want to practice psychology, you need a license. In order to obtain a license, you usually need to graduate from an APA-approved program in psychology.

Courses that might not transfer

Even when you transfer from one accredited college to another, every course you took in school might not transfer. Even if a course does transfer, there is no guarantee that it will be usable in your new degree program.

Here is a list of the common reasons that course credits might not transfer:

1. **Poor Grades.** Courses in which you received low grades generally will not transfer. Most colleges require a C or a C+ to accept a course for transfer. In most cases that means that a C- will not transfer.

2. **Transfer Limits.** All colleges limit the number of credits they will allow to be transferred toward a degree program. Some highly selective schools do not accept any transfer credits. However, most colleges usually allow a maximum of sixty semester hours, or two years of full-time study, to be transferred into a degree program. There are even some colleges that allow students to transfer a maximum of ninety credits, or three years of full-time study, into their degree program. Any previously earned credits in excess of the college's transfer limit will not be accepted.

3. **Religious courses.** Secular (non-religious) colleges generally do not accept religious courses taught by colleges with a religious affiliation, but will accept religious courses taught by other secular schools. For example, George Washington University would not accept a theology course taught at The Catholic University of America for transfer, but would accept a Comparative Religions course taught at the University of Maryland. On the other hand, any Catholic col-

lege in the country will accept a religion class taught at The Catholic University of America.

4. **Technical Courses.** Courses of a technical nature are difficult to transfer even when taken at an accredited college or university. If they are not offered by the school you are transferring to, then you probably will not receive credit for them. The key factors that determine acceptance are the nature of the course, the instructor's qualifications, and whether or not it is offered by the new institution. For example, if you took flying lessons at a certain university and then proceeded to transfer to a college without a flight school, you probably would not get credit for your flight training at the new university. You might have taken word processing at a junior college or secretarial school but might not receive credit for it when you transfer to a four year college. However, if you took Chinese at one university and transferred to another that did not offer it, you most likely would get credit because the Chinese language is considered to be of an academic rather than technical nature.

5. **Course Level.** Universities will not accept courses that are below the lowest level course they teach in a certain area. For example, if the lowest level math course a university teaches is precalculus, transfer credits will not be awarded for college algebra.

6. **Course Downgrading.** Credit could also be lost if a university downgrades your course. When downgrading occurs, a university awards credit for a course, but not as many credits as you were originally awarded. For example, you might have earned four credits for a course in Shakespeare at your first institution, but were awarded only three credits for it at your new institution since Shakespeare is a three credit course there.

7. **Not Applicable to a Degree Program.** Transfer credits can also be lost when changing majors. Courses might not be accepted because they do not apply to the major. For instance, if a student was applying to a School of Business but previously majored in Education, a university may decide not to accept the Education classes. At another school the credit may be accepted, but not applied toward the new

major. Students in this case will graduate with more than the required number of courses.

Non-Accredited Colleges

An institution that is not accredited doesn't mean the institution is of poor quality. Acquiring accreditation is a complex process and a few reasons a college may not acquire accreditation, besides failure to meet minimum standards, could be because it is a new school or simply chooses not to apply. But earning credits from a non-accredited school does mean that you will have more trouble transferring these credits to another school. Colleges have no way of ascertaining whether students who went to non-accredited schools meet or exceed minimum academic standards.

When deciding whether to award credit to a transfer student, admissions officers at accredited colleges consult *Transfer Credit Practices of Designated Educational Institutions,* published by the American Association of Collegiate Registrars and Admissions Officers. This book lists every college, university, and educational institution in the United States and its accreditation status. If the school is regionally or professionally accredited, it is listed here. In order for an admissions counselor from a regionally accredited college to accept credits from another college, it also must be a regionally accredited school. If the previous college has professional or technical accreditation, but does not have regional accreditation, transfer credits will not be accepted. The only schools that will accept credits for transfer from a school that does not have regional accreditation are other schools without regional accreditation.

If you went to a school that wasn't accredited, you would be better off to transfer to a school with accreditation as soon as possible and absorb the credit loss. Credits earned at non-accredited colleges can be reearned indirectly. Through examinations like CLEP, PEP, or individual credit examinations, the credits you earned that were not transferred may be regained. If earning credit by examination is impossible, you may be able to recoup non-transferred credits by requesting life experience credit.

Foreign Academic Experience

Most foreign universities are chartered, standardized, and controlled by the Ministry of Education, a branch of their national governments. The Ministry of Education is responsible for assuring uniform education within a particular country but doesn't allow for comparisons to be made from one country to another. The problems of interpreting and translating credit from an institution outside the United States can be enormous. First, there is the language barrier. It might be uncomplicated to translate documents from Germany, France, or other European countries, but documents from less familiar countries can pose more serious problems. Translation does not insure that what is translated will be interpreted accurately. A second difficulty is determining the academic level of an institution. In many countries high schools are called colleges and technical schools are called universities. Even if the level of a university can be assured, it's difficult to grant credit for courses when no equivalent courses exist. Grading systems also vary tremendously from country to country and consequently it can be almost impossible to determine passing or *C* level performance.

In order to assist universities in making decisions regarding admission, placement, and credit awards for foreign students, four organizations distribute guidelines to colleges and universities in the United States.

- The Council on International Educational Exchange
- The National Council on the Evaluation of Foreign Student Credentials
- The National Association for Foreign Student Admissions
- The National Liaison Committee on Foreign Student Admissions

Decisions regarding admission or the award of credit are solely under the jurisdiction of each college and university.

If you want to have a foreign transcript evaluated, there are four private organizations that offer this service for a fee:

World Education Services
P.O. Box 745
Old Chelsea Station
New York, New York 10011
212-679-0626

Education International
403 West 115th Street
New York, New York 10025
212-662-1768

International Education Research Foundation
Credentials Evaluation Service
P.O. Box 24679
Los Angeles, California 90024
213-474-7313

International Consultants of Delaware
914 Pickett Lane
Newark, Delaware 19711
302-368-3018

The recommendations of these professional evaluators are highly regarded and accepted by most institutions. In fact, many colleges use such evaluation services when deliberating difficult transcripts. But just because one of these organizations recommends that your foreign courses be awarded sixty credits is no guarantee that you will receive sixty credits. Credits are awarded solely at the discretion of the new institution you'll be attending.

If the school you have decided to attend will not honor the recommended credit award, you might consider transferring to another college or university which will accept the recommended credit award. If by applying to a different school, you can retain sixty credits, it will probably be in your best interest to do so.

Non-University Credit

Colleges may award college credit for certain courses even though they were taken outside a college setting. Courses taught by the federal government, the military, professional organizations, and businesses could be eligible for college credit. Since thousands of non-university classes are taught annually throughout the United States, it is impossible for individual colleges to evaluate each one. In order to assist colleges in deciding which non-university courses to accept for credit, the American Council on Education (ACE) conducts regular evaluations of non-university courses.

The American Council on Education is a nonprofit, independent, nongovernmental body concerned with postsecondary education. The council convenes the leaders of educational institutions to improve the educational standards, policies, services, and procedures. One area of focus of the council is providing credit for non-university sponsored education. Over thirteen million people a year participate in formal instruction outside the university setting. The American Council on Education through its Program on Non-Collegiate Sponsored Institution (ACE/PONSI) and Military Evaluation Program assesses the content, level of difficulty, quality of instruction, and potential credit award of courses taught outside college and university settings nationwide and distribute the results free of charge to every accredited college and university in the nation. Over fifteen hundred colleges adhere to the recommendations of the American Council on Education.

The recommendations of the American Council on Education are contained in three books:

1. *The National Guide for Education Credit for Training Programs*
2. *The Guide to the Evaluation of Educational Experiences in the Armed Services*
3. *The Guide to Educational Credit by Examination*

Universities and colleges follow the recommendations contained in these guides to determine whether or not to award college credit for a particular experience.

The first guide, *The National Guide for Education Credit for Training Programs*, recommends college credits for non-collegiate sponsored instruction. Training provided by businesses, government agencies, proprietary schools, professional organizations, and labor unions are all eligible for college credit. Since the Program on Non-Collegiate

Sponsored Instruction began in 1974, over four thousand courses from 230 different non-collegiate institutions have received credit recommendations.

Here are examples of the major categories of training evaluated in this guide:

Businesses: Businesses provide training that is aimed at improving the technical skills, productivity, and management skills of the workforce. If you've taken courses at work, they could be eligible for credit. Organizations such as Chrysler, AT&T, Ford, and Pacific Bell have had their course offerings evaluated for college credit.

Government Sponsored Courses: Most government agencies teach courses, many of which have been evaluated for college credit. The United States Department of Agriculture, Federal Aviation Administration, and the Internal Revenue Service are just three federal agencies that have had their courses evaluated by the American Council on Education.

Proprietary Schools: Proprietary schools are institutions that operate for profit as differentiated from tax-exempt, non-profit private schools. If you want to find out whether or not a school where you have earned credits is a proprietary school, refer to the *Directory of Accredited Institutions of Post-secondary Education* published by the American Council on Education and available at university and public libraries. The Dale Carnegie Schools and the Sullivan Schools are two examples of proprietary schools whose courses have been awarded college credit.

Professional Organizations: Professional organizations sponsor local, regional, and national education programs to provide their membership with current information and introduce or improve skill level. The American Bankers Association's courses for tellers and bank managers were evaluated for credit award. The Professional Association of Diving Instructors offers a variety of courses on every level of scuba diving which were evaluated and recommended for credit.

Labor Unions: Labor unions offer courses to enhance the technical skills and employment opportunities for their members. The United Auto Workers, UAW, and the Electrical Workers Union are two examples of unions with courses that have received recommended credit awards. If you have taken courses that were not evaluated for credit, the organization which taught or sponsored the course may call the American Council on Education to request an evaluation of the course.

The second guide, *The Guide to the Evaluation of Educational Experiences in the Armed Services* gives recommended credit awards for courses taught by the military and for certain Military Occupational Specialties (MOS). If you have a particular MOS, the guide suggests awarding a certain number of credits and further breaks this total credit award into specific courses. Although the actual credit award is dependent on the academic goals of the student and the policies of the institution, the *Guide to the Evaluation of Educational Experiences in the Armed Services*, recommends specific credit awards to colleges and universities, which are usually followed.

The third guide, *The Guide to Educational Credit by Examination*, evaluates examination programs in terms of educational credit. Programs evaluated include the College Level Examination Program (CLEP), the State of New York Regents College Examination Program, American College Testing/Proficiency Equivalency Program (ACT/PEP), Defense Activity for Non-Traditional Support (DANTES), United States Department of State, and a variety of licensure or certification examinations such as the Registered Professional Court Reporter Examination and the Certified Professional Secretary Examination. The Credit by Examination Program attempts to ensure that credit offered by examination is equivalent to traditional college level study. *The Guide to Educational Credit by Examination* provides a summary of test content, college course equivalents, recommended passing scores, and recommended credit awards.

If you want to have a first hand look at these guides, check your local college library, or they might be available in the reference section of your public library. You may order the guides or request more information from:

The American Council on Education
One Dupont Circle, Suite 20
Washington, DC 20036-1163

The Center for Adult Learning and Educational Credentials, Henry A. Spille, Director

Program on Non-Collegiate Sponsored Instruction (ACE/PONSI), Lansing J. Davis, Director

Registries and Credit by Examination, Joan G. Schwartz, Director

Military Evaluations Program, Eugene J. Sullivan, Director

Obtaining Transfer Credit

The first step in obtaining transfer credit is to organize your past educational experience. Make a list of all college-level learning you have had. This worksheet will help you organize your educational experiences:

Educational Background
Accredited Institutions Attended:
List the educational institutions you have attended. You'll request transcripts from all of these institutions.

Name	Address	Dates	Credits

Non-Accredited Institutions:
Make a list of all the courses you've taken at non-accredited colleges and universities. You will try to retain these credits by re-earning them via examination or portfolio assessment. After you list each of these courses, see if there is an exam title offered by CLEP or PEP which covers the same content. If not, add the course to your life experience portfolio.

Course	Exam	Yes/No	Portfolio

Foreign University Credits:

List the foreign educational institutions you have attended. You'll request transcripts from all of these institutions.

Name	Address	Dates	Credits

Non-University Educational Credit:

Make a list of non-university experiences you have had. You'll submit evidence of these courses to your new school for evaluation with any other college transcripts.

At Work

Course Title	Institution	Dates	No.Hrs.

Military or Government Courses

Course Title	Institution	Dates	No.Hrs.

Proprietary School

Course Title	Institution	Dates	No.Hrs.

Professional Organizations

Course Title	Organization	Dates	No.Hrs.

Labor Unions

Course Title	Organization	Dates	No.Hrs.

Have Your Previous Educational Experience Evaluated

Your transcript is an official record of the college level work you have done. Your transcript lists the courses you have taken by name and number, the dates you took them, and the grade you received. At the end of each semester your transcript will give an accounting of hours you earned that semester, your semester grade point average as well as total hours earned and cumulative grade point average.

The abundance of typewriters, xerox machines, and computers make it easy for a student to change a single grade or fabricate an entire transcript. Consequently, schools will only accept official transcripts for evaluation as a proof of your educational background. An official transcript is a transcript that is sent directly from one university to another and bears the official seal of the institution.

Unofficial transcripts are reproduced copies of official transcripts. Because they do not bear the official seal, they cannot be used as proof of your educational background even though they provide a record of your education. Other unofficial methods of documenting your educational background are grade slips and program of study.

To request an official transcript, write the to registrar of each college or university you attended. You should give all the information necessary to identify your academic record such as maiden or other name you might have used, your social security number, and all dates you attended the school. Schools generally will not honor phone requests. Because of laws concerning release of personal information, they require your signature before releasing your transcript. You must write and include the transcript fee, which is different for each institution.

If you are transferring schools, you will want to have your transcript evaluated. You may request either a preliminary (tentative) evaluation or official evaluation. During a tentative evaluation, an admissions counselor will look over your records and give you some idea about which courses will be accepted for transfer credit. A tentative evaluation is an unofficial evaluation. Schools will not stand behind the transfer estimate statements made by an admissions counselor in a preliminary evaluation even though these statements are very likely accurate. There is no charge for a preliminary evaluation. You don't even have to be a registered student to request one. Just call the admissions office of the college you are considering and make an appointment to meet with an admissions counselor. Bring all your records with you. For an unofficial evaluation, an unofficial copy of your transcript is sufficient.

Besides your transcript, also bring any documents, certificates, or evidence of other non-collegiate education or training you have completed. Documents may include a series of courses in computer programming, accounting, or management skills received from your employer. Examples of certificates and licenses include an Airman's License issued by the Federal Aviation Administration, Open Water Diver Certificate (C-card) issued by the Professional Association of Diving Instructors, Nurses Aide Certificate or Certificate to Administer Medications issued by an approved state health organization, CPR certificate or life-saving certificates issued by the Red Cross, Chartered Life Underwriter (CLU) certificate issued by the American College of Life Underwriters, Realtor Certificate issued by the National Association of Realtors, and other similar documents you have that are professional credentials, which demonstrate your knowledge of a particular field.

A formal evaluation of your transcript will be conducted after you are admitted to a college. For the formal evaluation, you'll have to arrange for official copies of your transcript to be sent directly to the school you'll be attending. That college or university will evaluate your transcript and mail the results to you. You may be requested to send additional information, such as copies of course descriptions from the catalog, course syllabi, or letters from instructors documenting the course content.

When a school decides to accept courses for credit, further adjustments may still be made. Quarter hours may have to be translated to semester hours, or vice versa. Three quarter hours equal two semester hours. If a student earns fifteen quarter hours, that translates to ten semester hours. Sixteen semester hours would be equal to twenty-four quarter hours.

When Credits Are Denied

When students have their transcripts evaluated, they are often dismayed at the number of credits that are awarded. A student from an accredited university could find the thirty credits earned in the first year of junior college decreased to twenty credits. A student who earned sixty credit hours at an unaccredited Bible college might find no credits awarded for those two years of college work. It is important to remember that initial evaluation is conducted by the book; further credits may be awarded if you appeal.

The appeal process is a delicate matter. You want to confidently state your case without alienating the admissions department. If your transcript is evaluated and some credits are not transferred, the best way to be awarded the credit you want is to make an educational argument. Use the course catalog, syllabi, and copies of work you submitted to prove that the course you took was of similar caliber to a course taught at your new school. Talk about the format of the course, how many times a week it met, and what assignments were given. Provide the instructors' qualifications to prove the educational caliber of the course. Personal arguments such as, "I spent $10,000 for these credits," or "Without these credits it will take me five years to graduate," may elicit sympathy, but won't win you the credit award you want.

If your credits were received from a non-accredited university, appealing will probably prove to be of no avail. You'll have to try to recoup the credits that are denied via examination or life experience credit.

If your effort to earn credit for non-university work is denied, try to earn credit for the knowledge you gained indirectly. Assemble evidence of this experience and knowledge in your life experience portfolio, or take a CLEP or PEP examination that will award you credit for the knowledge you gained.

The Credit Bank System

If you have a complicated educational history, you may want to use the service of a credit bank. A credit bank is an evaluation and transcript service for people who want to consolidate their academic records. The credit bank compiles the credits a student has received from a wide variety of institutions and learning experiences and issues a single transcript in which all credits earned are listed in an easy to read fashion. The advantages of a credit bank is that it can make sense and order out of a complex educational past. Six categories of learning experiences can be deposited in a credit bank.

1. *Credits Earned at Colleges/Universities.* Courses taken at regionally accredited colleges and universities are eligible for credit. Courses taken pass/fail or for a grade, whether through correspondence courses or in residence qualify for credit.

2. *Credits Earned by Examination.* Credits earned by passing any of several national standardized proficiency exams including CLEP, PEP, or DANTES are accepted.

3. *Credits Earned in the Military.* Courses taken as part of military training and military occupational specialties are evaluated for credit.

4. *Credits Earned at Non-Collegiate Learning Experiences.* Courses and seminars offered by businesses or organizations are evaluated for credit.

5. *Pilot Training.* Licensed pilots will receive credit commensurate with their airman's license level.

6. *Special Assessment of Learning in Other Fields.* Prior formal or informal non-collegiate learning will be evaluated in a variety of ways including portfolio assessment, oral examination, or performance.

Credits from all six of these sources are consolidated on a single transcript. To request a consolidated transcript, write to the credit bank:

> **The Regents Credit Bank**
> **Cultural Education Center**
> **Albany, New York 12230**

Resources

Credit for Training Programs and Other Transfer Credits

American Council on Education *The National Guide to Educational Credit for Training Programs*. New York: Macmillan Publishing, 1991.

> The American Council on Education's Program for Non-Collegiate Sponsored Instruction (PONSI) publishes recommendations for academic credit for learning acquired through training programs sponsored by

non-collegiate organizations that do not grant degrees. These organizations include business and industry, labor unions, professional and voluntary associations, and government agencies. The results of PONSI course evaluations are published annually in The National Guide to Education Credit for Training Programs that lists over four thousand courses for 230 non-collegiate organizations that have received credit recommendations since 1974. The credit equivalencies in the Guide are recommendations; the actual determination of credit awarded is dependent on institutional policy. Although intended primarily for use by college and university administrators, a look at *The National Guide to Educational Credit for Training Programs* can give students ideas about which of their previous training might be eligible for college credit.

CHAPTER 7
EARN DOUBLE

You don't have to attend class to earn college credit. You can earn credit for a work-related project, learning a new job skill, or current volunteer or leisure activities. Cooperative education programs, internships, and independent study projects allow you to earn college credit outside of the classroom. This chapter explains how to use all these projects to your benefit and move more quickly toward your degree.

Cooperative Education Programs

If you are employed full time, you probably spend at least forty hours a week at work. Even if you only work part time, your job probably dominates much of what you do. Through a **cooperative education program,** you can earn college credit for the work you do at work. The time you spend at work is your class time and what you learn at work is the course content.

If you don't have a job, but would like to gain some on-the-job training and experience, a cooperative education program can also help you. Universities that have a cooperative education program will help you to find a part-time or full-time paid position and then award you college credit for working.

Most schools limit the number of credits you can earn through a cooperative education program. For example, at the University of Maryland University College, a maximum of fifteen cooperative education credits will be awarded. At American University you can earn up to eighteen cooperative education credits. Colleges and universities also limit the number of cooperative education credits you can earn in a single semester. For example, at the University of Maryland, University College, a maximum of six cooperative education credits per semester is allowed.

The number of class sessions required also varies from school to school. At some schools, no class sessions are required; at others, an orientation session may be required, while some others require you to attend regular class sessions.

There are two types of cooperative education projects: **Self-Developed** and **University Developed.** Both types offer college credits for current work experience; the main difference is who finds the position. **Self-developed cooperative education projects** are aimed at students who are currently employed and want to co-op in their current position. Self-developed cooperative education students get credits for new responsibilities in their existing job. If you are unemployed and would like to gain work experience, apply for a **university developed** cooperative education project. The cooperative education office keeps a list of current jobs in a variety of career fields that offer solid learning opportunities. The cooperative education office will try to match your needs and interests to its available jobs.

Advantages of Cooperative Education

There are numerous advantages to enrolling in a cooperative education program. First, you'll get a salary for what you do at work while earning college credits for what you are learning at work. Work pays double. Earning college credit is almost effortless. There are no lectures to attend or tests to take.

Cooperative education projects are individualized to meet your needs. The projects assigned are custom tailored to your workplace, job responsibilities, and abilities. Grades for your cooperative education program are based on your final project rather than on a final exam. Students, skittish about tests, can earn college credit and avoid the trauma of exams. One main reason for signing up for cooperative education credits is to earn college credits without doing a lot of extra work. Another equally important reason is to get a good grade. The lack of examinations and the opportunity to work on projects that are custom tailored to your interests increase the probability that the grades you earn by cooperative education will be *A*'s. The vast majority of cooperative education students do earn *A*'s for their work projects. If you simply do what is specified in your learning contract, you should receive an *A*.

Cooperative education programs also give students an opportunity to develop a personal relationship with a faculty member. Instead of listening to a lecture with thirty to three hundred other students, you will meet regularly with a faculty member and receive personal input on how to perform more effectively at work.

Although self-developed and university developed cooperative education programs have many common advantages, they also have benefits that are unique to each. For example, self-developed cooperative education programs give students an opportunity to look at their old job in a new way. With the assistance of a faculty member, they will learn to look at their organization differently, approach tasks in a variety of ways, learn new job functions, and increase their overall level of performance. Cooperative education programs will also improve relationships with supervisors. Working on a cooperative education project provides you with a link between a university and your workplace. Your supervisor will see you as a growing, learning member of the staff.

University developed cooperative education projects also have unique benefits. Students who have not worked before, or who have not worked for a long time, can enter the workplace through a cooperative education program. If you are considering a new career, a cooperative education project can give you the opportunity to try out a new career without an extensive job search. As a change from the drudgery of traditional classes, a cooperative education project lets you learn by doing.

The Process

1. Apply to the cooperative education program.
Most colleges have a cooperative education office or at least someone assigned to coordinate cooperative education programs campus-wide. The application process may be different for a self-developed versus a university developed cooperative education program.

The questions on an application for a university developed cooperative education project will focus on **finding** you a suitable job. The application will ask your career goal, your major, what courses you have had in your major, the type of position you are interested in, the number of hours a week you want to work, and the geographic location where you want to work. Although a cooperative education office might not be able to match exactly every request, they will take your request very seriously.

The questions on the application for a self-developed cooperative education project focus on the appropriateness of your current position to a cooperative education project. The application will ask the nature of your current position, how long you have held it, your most recent promotion, what new activities or responsibilities you expect to have, how these activities relate to your program of study, and why you think a cooperative education program will benefit you.

In order to be eligible for a self-developed cooperative education project, you must have a job that provides an opportunity for **new, college-level** learning. The key words in this sentence are "new" and "college-level." If you have programed a computer for the past five years, writing another routine program would probably not be considered new unless you can prove that this new program is a unique application of what you already know. If you work as a file clerk or as an auto mechanic and you are going to be taught a new filing system or repair procedure, these experiences would be considered "new" learning but not at the "college level." In order to qualify for a cooperative education program, a work project or new procedure must be both new *and* require application of college-level knowledge.

If you've just gotten a new job, been promoted, or have recently been assigned new responsibilities at your current position, then a cooperative education program would be of particular benefit to you.

If you don't have a job, but could obtain one on your own or through the cooperative education office, you could use this job to obtain college credit.

Besides evidence of significant new learning, some colleges and universities require that students applying for cooperative education credit have a minimum grade point average. Others allow any student in good standing to apply for cooperative education credit. Most schools also require some college experience before students may apply for cooperative education credit. In general, sophomore status—thirty credits of previous college experience—is required before you can apply for cooperative education credit. If you are entering a new school, you might need to earn a certain number of credits from that school before applying.

At some colleges, cooperative education programs start at the beginning of the semester, just like any other course. At other institutions, students have the option of starting their cooperative education project at any time during the semester. When the program begins can have a direct impact on when you need to apply. To be eligible to participate in a cooperative education program starting in the fall semester, you might need to apply in the spring. Cooperative education projects, no matter when they start, are usually of a set length. Typically, cooperative education programs are fourteen weeks long, but you may be able to get a faculty member to approve a ten- to twelve-week project. Longer projects are also possible, but should be avoided. Since your objective is to get your degree finished in one year, you should undertake projects that can be completed in the shortest time allowed.

2. **Find an acceptable job.** If you don't have a job, securing an acceptable and appropriate job is the first step toward becoming eligible for cooperative education credits. Look for a suitable position through the cooperative educa-

tion office, where a current list of job openings and co-op projects is maintained. You can also use a job you find on your own as the basis for a work-study project.

3. **Write a learning proposal.** Once you have a job, the differences between a self-developed and university developed cooperative education project essentially disappear. For both self-developed and university developed cooperative education projects, you must write a learning proposal and a contract, find a faculty sponsor, and discuss your proposed work project with the person, probably your immediate supervisor, who will supervise your work project.

The learning proposal is an overview of your cooperative education project and generally contains three parts: a description of your current job position, the co-op project, and your educational goals.

The **job description** includes where you work, your job title, your duties, and how long you have been in the position. To prove this position involves new learning, you will have to show how your current position is either a new position, a promotion, or involves a new project that consists of significant new learning.

The **co-op project** is a description of the specific job or task you plan to complete to earn credit for the learning you acquire from doing the project. Examples of cooperative education projects include writing a training manual for the clerks, developing a current events lesson for a group of nursery school students, or developing a new type of budget projection from current revenues.

The **educational goals** section of the proposal describes what you expect to learn from the cooperative education project. It translates the project described in section two of the proposal to new learnings. The proposal you write will be a major factor in determining the success of your cooperative education project. Many students select a topic that is too broad and consequently contains an excessive amount of extra work. Select a narrow and clearly defined project. A project such as "train clerical employees" is too broad. *Develop and conduct three, one-hour training sessions for the clerical staff* would be more suitable.

4. Find a suitable faculty sponsor. Once you've applied to the cooperative education program and have been accepted, select a faculty member to supervise your project. At some schools the cooperative education office will select a faculty member to work with you. At other schools, it's up to you to choose your own sponsor. Faculty members should be selected based on their departmental affiliation, area of expertise, their enthusiasm for your project, their personality, and your relationship with him/her. Generally, faculty members will only sponsor projects in their own area of expertise. For instance, a project based in an elementary school classroom would require an Education Department faculty member. The faculty that sponsors your project also determines which department will evaluate your project and award you credit. If you are thinking of earning a minor in psychology and the project you are considering would potentially be eligible for either psychology or education credit, select a professor from the Psychology Department so that the credit you earn could be used toward your minor.

Although it's the most important, departmental affiliation is not the only criteria for selecting a suitable faculty sponsor. Another key factor is the attitude of the faculty member toward the cooperative education program. Ask the cooperative education program office to recommend a faculty member who is committed to the cooperative education process. Faculty who have previously worked with a cooperative education student will be more receptive to helping you than a faculty member who might not agree with the cooperative education concept.

Finally, select a faculty member with whom you get along well. If all other factors are equal, pick the faculty member who is an easier grader. Some faculty members are notoriously hard graders. Others give a high percentage of A's. An easy grader can reduce your work load and help boost your grade point average. If there is a faculty member with whom you have a good working relationship, you can ask him/her to sponsor your cooperative education project.

5. Develop a learning contract. The learning contract is the cornerstone of a cooperative education program. A student in conjunction with their sponsoring faculty member develops a suitable learning contract which **specifically** states what the student must do to receive cooperative education credits. A complete contract should contain: a **behavioral objective,** "what the student will learn by completing the contract;" **a list of activities** to accomplish the goal; and **a list of written assignments** that prove the goal was accomplished. The contract should also contain a **schedule of meetings** between the faculty member and the student, **the number of credits** the student will receive, and a **timetable for completing the project**.

A wise student selects activities that can be completed at work rather than proposing extensive written assignments that must be completed at home. The concept of cooperative education is to use work time to earn college credit. If you select activities that must be developed and written at home, you have defeated the purpose of cooperative education credits.

6. **Meet with your employer.** Once you and your faculty sponsor develop a written contract, meet with the project supervisor at work to explain your cooperative education project. Normally, your project will be something that your supervisor has asked you to do. But if none of your regularly assigned duties qualify for a cooperative education project, suggest a project that would benefit both you and your employer. If your boss is skeptical, highlight the benefits of the proposed project. Explain what both of you will learn from the project. Remind your boss that a faculty sponsor serves as a free consultant to you, indirectly helps his organization, and will assure the quality of your work. If your boss does not grant you permission to complete the assigned task, ask if there is another acceptable project. It doesn't matter who initiates the project, it is only important that the project is acceptable to you, your supervisor, and your faculty sponsor.

7. **Submit required written material on time.** Once deadlines are established, try to meet them. As a cooperative education student you are a professional employee and consequently should submit all tasks in a timely man-

ner. If you anticipate a problem, call your faculty sponsor ahead of time.

A variety of written activities are required by faculty members for cooperative education projects including a project status journal, data collection and analysis, charts and graphs, lesson plans, a computer program, photographic documentation, a video tape or written paper. But, although all of these activities might seem interesting, some are inherently easier than others. A journal is easier to write than a paper, and a paper based on your experiences is easier to write than a paper that integrates your experience with previously written research. A video tape that documents your experiences could be fun to produce, but might also take a lot more time than a written record of your experiences. Lobby for assignments that take a minimal amount of time on your part. When trying to earn a college degree in short order, time is your primary consideration.

Sample Cooperative Education Programs

Cooperative education programs can work in all fields of study. Here are some examples of cooperative education programs that were successfully completed by other students.

One student was awarded three credits for working part-time at a nursery school. She developed a program with her faculty advisor in which she was responsible for teaching a few lessons to small groups of students. As part of her cooperative education program, she gathered age appropriate games and learning activities from books, wrote lesson plans, and evaluated the success of each lesson.

Another student, who worked full time at a state mental hospital as an aide, was awarded six credits for preparing a case study of a troublesome patient. As part of her project, she observed the patient, kept a detailed log of the patient's activities, developed an intervention program with the aid of her faculty sponsor to minimize the patient's disruptive activity, implemented the program, and evaluated its effectiveness in changing the patient's behavior.

Internships

When you participate in an internship, a college or university provides you with a work experience specifically selected for its educational value. You receive college credit for your learning from the work experience. Departments that are interested in offering internships develop an internship base from a variety of sources. Faculty members use their contacts in the field to develop an internship base. In addition, businesses and government agencies call colleges and universities to request interns because they can use students as a temporary, highly educated, less expensive labor source. If the internship pool based on faculty contacts and employer requests isn't sufficient, faculty members may call alumni to find internships for their students.

The value placed on internships differs from department to department. In certain departments, internships are considered so important that they are a required part of the degree program. In other departments, an internship may be recommended but not required. Other departments might not even offer internships. Radio and television degree programs usually require internships in which students work at actual television or radio stations. Psychology departments may also require internships to give students experience working with patients. Education departments generally offer a variety of internships from working as a teacher's aid to being assigned as assistant principal.

Internships are generally of limited duration, usually lasting for one semester and, at the most, for one year. An intern is specifically hired as a summer intern, a fall intern, or a spring intern. Student interns are not hired in a permanent position; the position only lasts a limited amount of time. Internships may be paid or unpaid. Interns are normally paid less than competitive rates since they are short-term trainees with the intent being to gain knowledge from the work experience.

An intern has both a university and field-based supervisor. The field supervisor assigns tasks and supervises your work on a daily basis. The role of the university supervisor is minimal. Regular meetings are generally scheduled only with the field supervisor, rather than the university supervisor. It is the field supervisor who assigns your grade. During an internship, the experience is the basis of the learning experience. Interns are generally not required to write a proposal, submit a learning contract, or write a paper. The only written assignment that is usually required is a daily journal that is submitted at the end of the internship.

Although similar to cooperative education projects, internships do differ from cooperative education projects in a number of ways. First, internships are generally administered by each individual department while cooperative education projects are centrally administered by an office in the university. Internships may be required in a specific degree program, while cooperative education programs are always ancillary to the degree program. While working as a temporary employee on a cooperative education project, you could be offered a permanent job with the company. A cooperative education project is based on working at a regular job and consequently paid at regular salary rates. Interns, if paid at all, are paid on a reduced salary scale.

The role of a university supervisor is different during an internship and a cooperative education experience. For a cooperative education experience, the university supervisor assigns your grade based on your weekly meetings and your written work. During an internship, it is the field supervisor who has primary responsibility for your development.

The focus of an internship and a cooperative education program are also different. During a cooperative education project, you earn credit for a project done as part of your work experience. The regular meetings with your university supervisor and a written summary of your project form the basis of your grade. During an internship, the entire work experience is the learning experience.

Comparison

Cooperative Education Programs	Internships
Administered by University	Administered by department
Optional	May be required
Paid	Paid, reduced or unpaid
Unlimited duration	Limited duration
University supervised	Field supervised
Project oriented	Experience oriented

Independent Study

If the school you are attending doesn't have a cooperative education program, you could work out a similar arrangement using the college program for independent study. One student wanted to earn college credit for coaching an elementary school basketball team, but since the position of coach was neither full-time nor paid, she did not meet the requirements of a cooperative education program as mandated by the university she was attending. Instead of giving up, she found a college faculty member who was interested in coaching and asked to do an independent study. They worked together to develop an independent study entitled Coaching Youth Sports. The student was required to write out practice plans, keep a journal of her reaction to practice sessions and readings, and write a short paper that summarized what she learned.

Independent study is a course without pre-designated content. The content of the course is whatever the student wants it to be. Independent study can best be described as designing your own course. Anything can be an independent study project, as long as a faculty member agrees. Find a faculty member you like and suggest an independent study project. Your project can be reading-based, project-based, or experienced-based.

The advantages of independent study are tremendous. First, you can study precisely what you want because you design the course to suit you. Next, you get to learn in the way that is best suited to your learning style. If you like to read, you can read, if you prefer to visit museums, you can do that too because your design not only determines the content of the course but also its format.

You also select the method of evaluation. You choose if you'd like to take a test, write a paper, or make a video presentation to demonstrate the knowledge you acquired as a result of your project. In fact, any method of evaluation is possible.

Independent study courses offer tremendous time savings. There are no regular class sessions, no commuting time, no weekly homework assignments. Generally, you meet with the instructor you select at the beginning of the semester to outline your proposal, meet once or twice during the semester to provide a progress report, and meet at the end of the semester to hand in the assignments. The work load is much lighter in an independent study course than in most courses because you developed it.

Independent study courses are also an easy way to boost your grade point average. If you decide to design an independent study course, here are the steps to follow.

1. Brainstorm possible ways to earn independent study credit.

Think of things you could do, books you could read, or other ways you could earn independent study credits. Pick things you have a strong interest in, strong background in, or things you either have to do or want to do. If you're going to do something anyway, there's no reason you shouldn't earn credit for it.

For example, if you have a strong interest in marine mammals (whales, dolphins, and the like), you could propose to read several books or research papers on the subject, discuss your findings with your faculty advisor and write a summary report. If you have a strong background in Italian culture because you grew up in an Italian family, you could do a project on the differential treatment of male and female children in the Italian family. You would accomplish this by interviewing Italian-Americans and weaving their experience with that of your own. If you have to train your dog in obedience, you could get credit for that as well. And if you are planning a one-week vacation to England, you could even get credit as a result of your trip.

2. *Select a title for the course you are proposing.*

Make the title sound appropriate for college work so that even if what you are doing is simple, the title makes it sound difficult. If you want to write a paper on your childhood, call it "The Differential Treatment of Male and Female Children in the Italian Family" rather than "Growing Up in an Italian Family." Using another example, if you're going to train your dog, don't title your project "How I Trained Rover," but rather "Canine Response to a Systematic Behavior Modification Program." If you are planning a trip to England, your proposal could best be titled "The Architecture of English Cathedrals" or "British Pubs as A Mechanism of Social Integration," rather than "My Trip to England."

3. *Decide how you are going to accomplish your goal.*

In this section of your proposal, you describe the process. What are you going to do to accomplish your goal? If you are traveling through England on a vacation, but at the same time you intend to study the architecture of England's famous cathedrals, explain the process. Explain each of the specific things you will do to learn about the cathedral, such as interviewing tour guides about the cathedrals, reading about Gothic architecture, photographing the cathedrals, and making comparisons between the cathedrals visited.

If you're going to train your dog, outline specifically what you're going to do such as attend weekly training classes with your dog, have two daily thirty-minute training sessions with the dog, keep a daily journal of your dog's progress and responses, and read a book on dog training.

4. *Determine the evaluation process.*

At the end of the semester, you must submit something to your faculty sponsor to prove you've accomplished your stated goal. What you submit could be in the form of a journal, a scrapbook, a videotape, a paper, a license, certificate, or any combination of the above. What you decide to do should be determined both by your project and by what type of work you like to do. For example, if you trained your dog, you might want to submit your journal and a paper that includes a summary of what you've learned integrated with your readings. If you studied English cathedrals, you might want to submit a scrapbook, which includes photos and architectural descriptions of the cathedrals you visited along with a brief summary paper highlighting their significance.

5. *Determine the number of credits you want.*

Most colleges and universities set a limit on the number of credits that can be earned from an independent study course as well as the total number of independent study credits that can be used toward a degree program. Anywhere from three to six credits is the usual limit for an individual course, from six to twelve for the total number of independent study credits that can be applied toward a degree. Always ask for more credits to be awarded than you think your project deserves. If you think the course you've planned is worth three credits, ask for six as long as six is within the college's accepted limits. If you only ask for three credits, that's all you'll be able to get, but if you ask for six credits, you just might get them.

6. *Select a faculty member to supervise your project.*

Any faculty member of a college or university is eligible to supervise an independent study. The faculty member you pick will be based on your topic and their willingness to supervise your project. Let's look at the topics you brainstormed and identify which department you should go to for an appropriate faculty sponsor. For a project on whales and dolphins, look for a sponsor in the biology department. If you want to focus on animal intelligence, look for a sponsor in the psychology department. If you're going to train your dog, try finding your sponsor in the psychology or education departments. For the trip to England project, select a faculty member from the art department or history department if you're going to focus on the architecture of the cathedrals. If you are going to focus on life in British pubs, pick a faculty member in the sociology department. If your project will deal with language differences between American English and British English, look for a sponsor in the English or speech department.

Once you decide which is the best department to find a faculty sponsor, you have to pick a specific faculty member with whom to work. The faculty member you pick is very important to your earning the maximum number of credits and receiving the highest grade. A picky faculty member can turn three hours of an easy *A* into a project that is difficult. Find a faculty member that has an interest in your project who has a reputation for being an easy grader.

7. *Present your idea to a faculty member.*

Make an appointment to meet with the faculty member of your choice. Before the meeting, write a one-page proposal that summarizes the goals, activities, and evaluation process of your project. Armed with your proposal, ask the faculty member if he or she would consider sponsoring an independent study project. If the answer is yes, present your proposal. Explain your idea briefly before you present your written proposal. Most faculty members will accept your proposal if it is a sound one, but some will make a few minor modifications. They might suggest that you narrow your goals, add an activity, read a specific book, or modify the evaluation. Go along with these suggestions as long as they don't seem overwhelming. Remember an independent study is a way to earn an easy *A*. If the project becomes too involved, you may want to consider taking a regular course. After you've agreed upon what you're going to do, state how many credits you want. If you ask for six credits, some faculty members will say okay, others will say they really don't think your project as proposed is equivalent to six credits (equal to ninety hours of time). Counter their statement with, "I really planned to earn six credits. Is there anything I could add to the project to make it worth six credits?" More often than not, your faculty sponsor will suggest a small addition that will be worth three extra credits.

Sample Independent Study Proposal #1

Title: "Canine Response to A Systematic Behavior Modification Program"

Goals:

1. Use systematic behavior modification to teach a dog basic commands (sit, come, stay, fetch, heel, lie down).

2. Compare the relative effectiveness of approval rewards and food rewards.

3. Determine whether behaviors initially taught using food rewards effectively remain when the food reward is removed.

Activities:

1. Read a book on dog training.

2. Attend weekly training sessions with dog at a licensed dog school with a professional dog trainer and a group of other students.

3. Establish two 15-minute training sessions per day. Each training session will target three different behaviors. During the first session, the dog will receive training to sit, heel, and fetch. During the second session of the day, the dog will receive training to lie down, come, and stay. The first training of the day will use food rewards. The second training session of the day will use approval rewards.

4. Keep a daily journal of training sessions that includes your observations and reactions to the training process. Keep a record of how quickly the dog learns the various target behaviors. Compare how quickly the dog learns behaviors when the trainer uses approval rewards with behaviors learned with food rewards.

5. During the last two weeks of training, eliminate food rewards and use only approval rewards. Compare how the dog responds to behaviors that were initially taught using food rewards and those that were taught using approval rewards.

Evaluation:

1. Write a summary paper that integrates the information learned from the readings, the obedience classes, and one-on-one training sessions.

2. Submit a copy of your journal.

Sample Independent Study Proposal #2

Title: "Margaret Mead: Her Life and Her Work"
Goals:
1. Review the life of Margaret Mead.
2. Understand the significance of her work.
Activities:
1. Read Margaret Mead's autobiography, *Blackberry Winter*.
2. Read Margaret Mead's first book, *Coming of Age in Samoa*.
3. Read a biography of Margaret Mead.
4. Interview three anthropologists regarding the significance of Dr. Mead's work.
5. Interview Dr. Mead's daughter, Professor Bateson, at George Mason University.
Evaluation:
Write a fifteen to twenty-page paper summarizing the interviews and readings.

Resources

Cooperative Education Programs

Lutzker, Marilyn *Research Projects for College Students: What to Write across the Curriculum*. Westport, CT: Greenwood Press, 1988.

Research Projects for College Students provides project ideas which are offered as a starting points for designing individualized projects to meet specific needs. These ideas are presented as suggestions to help students develop meaningful research projects that require active planning. It guides students doing research projects on how to sleuth in the sources for data and to sift through material and ideas.

CHAPTER 8
THE OLD-FASHIONED
WAY UPDATED

After you've gathered together your existing and potential credits from every other source, it's time to tackle some conventional courses. Because conventional courses take more time and effort than earning credit by examination or life experience, **The One Year to a College Degree Program** advises taking as few conventional classroom courses as possible.

When conventional courses are taken, they should be selected carefully with the help of your advisor to assure that they meet the requirements for your degree and take the least amount of time and effort possible. This chapter will help you work effectively with your advisor to select courses that offer maximum benefit to you. This chapter also will help you understand the advantages and disadvantages of the different types of courses offered at most colleges and select those that are best suited to your needs.

Your Advisor

It takes at least 120 credits to earn a bachelor's degree, but not just any 120 credits. You must satisfy the college's requirements for a degree: major requirements, minor requirements, general education requirements, residency requirements, upper level course requirements, lower level course requirements, and grade point average requirements. Although you're ultimately responsible for scheduling your program and assuring that you meet all the graduation requirements, an advisor can be a big help. It will be much harder for you to plan the quickest and easiest way to a degree without an advisor. The role of the undergraduate advisor is filled by a variety of personnel at colleges and universities. At some colleges, undergraduate faculty assume the responsibility of advising undergraduate students. Upon admission to the college, students are assigned an advisor, a faculty member in their major field of study, to help them plan their program and register for courses. At other schools graduate students are assigned the role of advisor. These graduate students generally receive free tuition and a stipend to advise students. These graduate student advisors relieve faculty of the additional workload of advising undergraduate students. Graduate student advisors may be based in a single department, or asked to serve the entire college community.

The importance given to the advisor varies from college to college. At some schools the advisor is an integral part of the students' education. Students are not allowed to register for classes without consulting their advisor. To assure consultation, the advisor's signature is required on all registration materials. At other schools the advisor's services are optional, and students are allowed to register without the services of an advisor.

But no matter who serves as your advisor and what the regulations are concerning advisor consultations, advisors can make your undergraduate career easier. Advisors can help you interpret the catalog, the key to planning your program successfully. As long as you remain an active student, the catalog that is current for the first semester you enroll is the college's contract with you throughout your college career. Updated degree requirements after your first semester will have no bearing on your degree program or graduation requirements since they were not in effect when you initially enrolled.

Besides interpreting the catalog, advisors can answer many of your questions including, "What courses should I take?" "How many of my credits will transfer?" "Which courses should I take together?" If your advisor cannot answer a particular question, he or she will find someone who can. For example, if your advisor is stumped by a financial aid question, he or she can direct you to someone in the financial aid office who can help you.

An advisor generally has limited authority. The advisor is there to give advice, not to render policy or grant exceptions to current policy. For example, if you want permission to take one required course instead of another, at most colleges you must get such permission from the chairman of the department in which you want to make the change—not from your advisor. If knowledge of a second language is required for graduation and you want to petition to have your skill in sign language or a computer language count for a second language, instead of the traditional foreign language, your advisor cannot grant this waiver.

Don't think advisors are powerless. Though they can't help you reduce the number of credits to earn your degree, they can point you to the quickest and easiest ways to earn credits.

They can't sign a wavier and get you into a course that is closed, but they can call the professor teaching the course and explain why you need to be in the course.

They generally can't give you permission to substitute one course for another, but they can help you to write your petition to ask for such permission.

They can't change the grade in a course after you earn it, but they can tell you what professors are notoriously easier graders.

They can't design a major especially for you, but they can tell you which majors have the least requirements or show you ways to juggle the credits you've earned to get maximum benefit.

Tips for Working with an Advisor

It's important to have a good working relationship with your advisor. An advisor who is on your team can be a great asset. Here are a few tips that, if followed, will assure that you get the most out of your meetings with your advisor.

1. **Request the same advisor each time.** Some schools

will assign you a particular advisor, while at other schools you will be expected to go to an advising office and meet with one of several advisors, similar to going to a walk-in clinic. If the latter is the case, find one you work well with and request that same advisor each time you make an appointment. Meeting with several different advisors will only confuse you and slow down your progress toward a degree.

2. **Set an Appointment.** Advisors are notoriously busy. If you just drop in during office hours, your time may be limited to a few minutes. Other students will also be vying for time and your advisor might feel rushed to answer your questions in short order. But if you set up an appointment and request a half hour block of time, that half hour will be all yours. Students waiting in the hallway will be told your advisor has an appointment and will be available when your appointment time is up.

3. **Write out your questions ahead of time.** You should organize the time you schedule to meet with your advisor. Although it's nice to spend time getting to know your advisor on a personal level, it's also important to use the block of time productively. Trying to earn your college degree at record pace means you have little time to schedule frequent meetings with your advisor. The meetings you do schedule should answer as many of your questions as possible. Write down your questions ahead of time. Your advisor will appreciate your effort, since it will save everyone time.

4. **Bring materials with you.** When you meet with your advisor for the first time, bring your permanent school records, such as copies of transcripts, copies of scores from college level examinations, and proof of military service training. On subsequent visits, bring the information, materials, and documents you developed during your last advising visit, such as your program of study and class schedule. Keep all your advising materials together in a folder so that they are ready whenever you need them.

5. **Be respectful.** The key to getting along with and thereby getting the most benefit from an advisor is to show respect. Request rather than demand; clarify rather than as-

sume; pursue rather than pound. Being courteous begets courtesy.

6. Get it in writing. You *and* your advisor will plan a program of study and work out your schedule. If you also get permission, either through or from your advisor, to take one course instead of another, to take courses out of sequence, to enroll in courses at another school because they are not offered at your school, or to use certain courses to satisfy degree requirements, get the permission in writing. Make sure your advisor signs and dates all changes.

When it comes time to graduate, someone other than your advisor will check to make sure that you have fulfilled all of the graduation requirements. If something has been omitted or is out of the ordinary on your record, you may not graduate. Explaining to the records office that your advisor, who may have left the college in the meantime, gave you permission to substitute astronomy for biology will be of little value unless you have it in writing. Trying to receive written permission after the fact will be of no help because your advisor might not remember granting such permission or has moved to a new job so that you can not find him or her.

7. Send a follow-up letter. Each time you meet with your advisor, send a follow-up letter to your advisor that summarizes your meeting. Also be sure to thank your advisor for his or her time and help. This follow up letter is the foundation to your success. It serves as your verification of what you thought happened at the meeting. If your advisor doesn't agree with what you've written, he or she can correct your letter. No response from your advisor indicates implicit agreement with what you wrote.

Selecting Courses

College professors have fought hard for academic freedom, the freedom to teach their courses however they want. They now have total freedom to select which books to use, the assignments required, and the number and type of tests they administer. The same course taught by two different professors can be very different in content, difficulty, and workload. Contrast this with the way things are done in high school, where books are ordered school-wide if not system-wide and every student taking geometry, American history, or Spanish I is taught the same content in ostensibly the same way.

Selecting courses is an important factor in your success since the same course taught by two different instructors can essentially be two different courses. Choose the easiest courses that will satisfy your degree requirements. You are trying to earn your degree in as short an amount of time as possible. You need to find "cake" courses, courses in which minimum effort will earn you an *A* or a *B*. The difficulty of the course is more important than the content of the course. If you need a history course to graduate, pick the easiest one. Don't select Russian History because it's difficult, even though you think it will be the most interesting. In the **One Year to a College Degree Program,** speed and ease are synonymous.

Several factors determine whether a course is easy or hard. The following five questions should help you evaluate the difficulty of a course.

1. Is minimal reading involved?

College courses vary in the amount of reading required. It is not unusual to find an English course that requires from five to eight books, or a history course that requires students to read one hundred to two hundred pages a night. When you are taking several courses at a time and are employed full time, extensive reading can cut heavily into your allotted study time. Look for courses that require a minimum amount of reading.

2. Is the instructor an easy grader?

Instructors differ in the way they grade papers. Research repeatedly has shown that the same paper will receive grades ranging from an *A* to an *F* depending on who's grading it. Certain professors are notoriously easy graders and give almost every paper an *A* or a *B*. Other professors are extremely critical and hesitate to give even a stellar paper an *A* or a *B*.

It's important for you to find the professors who are easy graders to make your task of getting through college in one year less burdensome with the same result.

3. Are written assignments minimal?

Classes vary in the number and extensiveness of written assignments. A single three-credit class may require no papers, one comprehensive paper, several short papers or several comprehensive papers. Written assignments are time consuming. Select classes that require minimal written work. Don't count the number of papers required, but rather look at the number of written pages required. Two four-page papers are less work than one ten-page paper. Two ten-page papers are more work than one fifteen-page paper.

4. What are the testing requirements?

Instructors also differ in their testing practices. Some instructors quiz the students on a weekly basis to make sure they keep up with the class material. Others administer three or four major exams; still others base a student's grade on a midterm and final exam or only on a final exam. In order to graduate quickly, you should select courses with minimal testing requirements. On the positive side, extensive testing may force you to keep up with the class on a weekly basis, but it also forces you to attend class regularly and devote an extensive amount of time to a single class when you are taking several other classes that need your time and attention.

5. Am I good at the subject matter?

Some classes play into your natural strengths more than others. Other classes, no matter how easy, are not suited for you. Math classes generally require minimal reading and no written assignments and, for people with math aptitude, they can be an easy way to earn credit. However, for students with little or no math aptitude, math classes can be a nightmare. Assess your academic strengths and weaknesses and select classes that are best suited for you.

Tips for Selecting Courses

It's important to select classes that play to your strengths, are taught by an easy grader, and have minimal reading, writing, and testing requirements. All the classes you take might not meet all five of these requirements, but it is important to search for easy classes that will make your goal of a college degree in one year easier to achieve. There are lots of ways to find out which classes are the easiest without actually taking them. Here are a few tips:

TIP #1: Plan to attend the first class of each course you listed as a possibility.

At the first class session, each instructor hands out a syllabus which outlines the course material, reading assignments, required written assignments, and testing practices. Reviewing the syllabus is an easy way to find out the level of work required, whether or not attendance is mandatory, whether late assignments are accepted, and the instructor's teaching style.

There is nothing to stop you from attending the first class of several different courses even if you don't intend to register for them all. If you need to take a particular course or a course in a particular subject area, shop around. Attend several classes taught by a variety of faculty members, so that you will be able to select the class that will give you the highest grade with the least work.

TIP #2: Ask for a copy of the course syllabus.

If you can't attend the first class of a course you're interested in, stop by the professor's office and ask for a copy of the syllabus. Most professors have the syllabus ready before the first day of class, and you may be able to get a preview of what's required. Some professors don't like to give out their syllabus before the first day of class, but you can pick it up any time after that. Just say you are interested in signing up for the class, you missed the first class and need a copy of the syllabus. Only a rare professor will refuse.

TIP #3: Visit the campus bookstore.

Another way to select easy classes, though not as reliable as the class visits, is by visiting the campus bookstore. You can "shop" for easy classes at the bookstore by looking for those classes with the least amount of required reading.

Most college bookstores allow students to walk through the aisles where the books are organized by course. Each course has a one page summary sheet or shelf card that lists both the required and recommended books. When picking a course by the reading required, ignore the list of recommended books. Pick courses with the easiest and shortest list of required readings. Don't just look at the number of books, also look at the books themselves to compare the total number of pages.

TIP #4: Talk to other students to find out which classes are easy classes.

Ask students you meet during registration, in your classes, during orientation, or anywhere else, if they have taken any easy classes. Ask, if they've taken any classes on your possible course list, for their opinion of the easiest professors and classes. Students are a good source of information about the reputation of different courses.

TIP #5: Your advisor may also be able to recommend courses that meet your specific requirements.

Advisors talk to lots of students about their classes and they get an indirect picture of what goes on in class. They also see the report cards of their advisees. A helpful advisor can suggest easy courses.

TIP #6: Many students select courses by the instructor.

If you previously had an instructor that you liked, who was not too demanding in terms of requirements, and was an easy grader, sign up for other courses with the same instructor. Professors generally like to see a familiar face on the first day of class.

TIP #7: It's also possible to ask the instructor whether the course you're interested in is easy or not.

Simply explain that you'll be taking a heavy load this semester and you won't have the time to take a course that requires a lot of reading or a lot of written work. Instructors generally will be candid. They know the relative difficulty of the courses about which you're debating taking compared

to other courses they teach and to other courses on campus.
If they've taught the course before, they probably have a good
idea how many hours a week an average student needs to
spend to get an *A*.

TIP #8: Examine instructors' grade sheets.

At the end of each semester, most instructors post grade
sheets on their office door or on the bulletin board. These
grade sheets list the social security numbers of the students
in the class and the grades they received. These grade sheets
are a very reliable way to find instructors who are easy graders. For example, if you need to take a history course, just
walk down the hallway where the offices of the history department faculty members are located and scan the grade
sheets. Write down the names of the courses and faculty
members where a preponderance of *A*'s were given. Look
up these courses in the catalog to see if you are eligible to
take them.

TIP #9: The department secretary is a good source of insider information.

If you need to take a course in a specific department,
talk informally with the department secretary. The secretary
knows more about the faculty members in a specific department than anyone else, including which faculty members are
popular with students, which are easy graders, which have
interesting classes, and which are respected by other faculty
members for being knowledgeable in their field. The departmental secretary garners information from a variety of
sources. By listening to students criticize or praise specific
instructors and from working with the faculty on a daily basis,
the secretary forms an informal opinion regarding various
faculty members. The secretary is also privy to such confi-
dential information as student evaluations of faculty, grade
sheets, and personnel files. Getting information about a
specific course or faculty member from the secretary is easy.
Just ask, "I'm thinking about taking a course from Dr.
Whatizname. Do you know if he's a hard grader?" Or ask,
"Have you heard anything about Business Law?"

TIP #10: Sign up for classes that you have a strong background in.

Another way to take easy classes is to sign up for classes that you have a knack for, a strong background in, took in high school, studied through a work training program, or had been non-transferable credits. Even though you may qualify for upper level credits, register for lower level classes first. For example, even though you qualify for calculus because you had pre-calculus in high school, sign up for pre-calculus again to earn five easy college credits. Don't always sign up for the hardest courses. Easy courses earn the same number of credits as difficult courses.

TIP #11: Take classes Pass-Fail.

Many colleges allow students to take classes pass-fail. Instead of receiving a letter grade on their report card, students receive a *P* or an *F*. Grades of a *C* or above are awarded a Pass, and grades below a *C* are recorded as a Fail. Colleges generally limit the number of Pass-Fail classes a student can take. Some even limit which classes may be taken Pass-Fail. For example, a college may only allow students to take thirty credits Pass-Fail and these may not be in the student's major.

Take as many classes as you can as Pass-Fail. Taking a difficult class as Pass-Fail makes it easy, and taking an easy class as Pass-Fail makes it a snap.

TIP #12: Search out easy courses.

If you are not having any luck finding easy courses using tips #1-11, here are a few more places to look. There are plenty of easy classes, sometimes called "gut courses," on almost every college campus. These classes will generally serve as electives and should provide some personal benefit to you either now or later on in your life. The following list of courses are generally easy at all colleges and universities.

1. **Ceramics (Art)** Ceramics requires very little artistic talent to master the basics. Earn three credits and leave the class with a few new dishes.

2. Drawing (Art) Although drawing takes more talent than ceramics and print making, most students enrolled are not budding Picasso's. An art course can provide a good break from an overly academic schedule, but be careful because some art courses require extensive amounts of time.

3. Human Sexuality (Psychology, Health) Most adults know much of the material covered in an undergraduate human sexuality course. If you don't, it's really not hard to learn about the "birds and the bees" on a college level. Besides, most students find the reading material fascinating.

4. Voice and Articulation (Speech) Learn how to "correctly" pronounce the words you already know how to pronounce but without your regional accent.

5. Chorus (Music) Most people can sing well enough to sing in a college chorus. There's no homework involved, and it's a good place to make new friends.

6. Introduction to Astronomy (Astronomy) If you must have a science course to satisfy your degree requirements, astronomy is probably the easiest. Astronomy generally doesn't have a lab, and most astronomers are highly philosophical.

7. Parenting (Psychology, Human Development) If you already have children, most of what you'll learn in this course is not new. If you don't have children yet or your children are young, there will be future benefits from what you learn.

8. Personal Career Planning and Development Although not offered at all colleges, this course helps students select a future career direction for their life.

9. Introduction to Computers (Computer Science) Learn what a computer is and how it works. Easy to learn as well as essential knowledge for all college graduates.

10. Introduction to Computer Software (Computer Science) Learn how to use computer programs for word processing, spreadsheets, and other basic computer functions. A snap course for anyone who already uses a computer and essential for anyone who doesn't.

11. Elementary School Mathematics (Education) This course reviews all the math you learned in elementary school. For anyone with a modicum of mathematics talent, it's a snap.

12. Elementary Mathematics Methods (Education) This course is intended to train future teachers how to teach mathematics. Loaded with games, activities, and manipulatives, most students find it fun and easy.

13. Art Methods (Education) This course teaches you how to teach art in elementary school. Learn how to make potato stamps, papiermache, and a variety of other projects to earn an easy *A*.

14. Business Writing (English, Business) In a business writing course you earn easy credit for improving the way you write letters, memos, proposals, and reports. Business writing sharpens skills you already have or those you learned in high school.

15. Sign Language (Communications) Learn how to communicate with the deaf using sign language. Almost every student who takes this course loves it. Some colleges classify sign language as a "language."

16. Adult Development (Psychology) Learn about yourself now and in your later years.

17. First Aid (Health) Learn how to administer first aid and earn an advanced first aid certificate card from the American Red Cross. You spend class time putting on bandages, giving CPR to dummies, and learning to identify different types of injuries. This course is valuable and easy.

18. Safety Education (Health) This course teaches students to teach others about safety education, such as fire safety, electrical safety, and safety in the home.

19. Women's Health (Health) Women generally find this course easy since they know most of the information that's taught in it. The course is practical and easy.

20. College Algebra (Mathematics) This is the easiest mathematics course most colleges offer. If you have to take a math class, this is it. If you don't need a math course, you might still want to sign up for college algebra; it's basically a review of high school Algebra II.

21. Introduction to Music (Music) If while you were growing up you learned to play a musical instrument, this course shouldn't be too hard. You'll relearn the scales, notes, chords, and other musical concepts.

22. **Principles of Real Estate (Business)** If you need a business course, this is generally one of the easier ones. At the completion of the course at most colleges and universities, you are eligible to receive a real estate license. Even if you're not interested in being a real estate agent, the information taught is helpful to any student thinking of buying or selling a house.

23. **Sex Roles (Psychology, Sociology)** How are men and women different? How much of these differences are genetic? How much is due to training? In this course you'll find the answer to these and many other questions.

24. **Interpersonal Communication (Psychology, Education)** Not available everywhere, this course will help you communicate more effectively with your spouse, children, co-workers, and friends. Generally taught in a laboratory style, most students find the class sessions fun and fascinating.

25. **Introduction to Acting (Theatre)** A course that is generally taught as a combination of lecture, demonstration and laboratory activity, most students find this course fun and interesting.

Course Formats

Adult learners are the fastest growing and largest college population. In 1991 over two million adults over the age of thirty-five were enrolled in college. Colleges and universities, aware of the changing demographics of their student population, have changed the format of their classes. Thirty years ago college courses were taught much like high-school courses, in one hour blocks, several times a week. Two credit classes met for two one-hour blocks, three credit classes met for three one-hour blocks, and five credit classes met for five one-hour blocks. But adult students who work or are otherwise busy during the day were unable to attend classes scheduled in this way. In order to accommodate adult students, colleges implemented a variety of new class formats.

The variety of class formats will be described, and the advantages and disadvantages of each will be discussed. Not all colleges offer all types of classes, but the following descriptions will give you a list of the possibilities.

Night Classes

Originally, college classes met during the day, but now night classes are as common as day classes. In addition, night classes meet once a week to reduce the commuting time of adult students. Most colleges teach night classes in two time blocks in order to maximize offerings. For a three-credit class, the traditional time blocks are 4 to 7 P.M. and 7 to 10 P.M. Other colleges use a slightly later schedule, 5 to 8 P.M. and 8 to 11 P.M. Classes in this format run from fourteen to sixteen weeks.

This format, three hours once a week after traditional work hours, is the most common class format offered by colleges that cater to adult students. These class sessions are taught using a variety of activities, including lectures, class discussions, group activities, student presentations, films, and guest speakers. Assignments vary from instructor to instructor but generally include a mid-term exam, final exam, and several papers or homework assignments.

The advantage of this format is that you have regular contact with an instructor. In courses that students find difficult—like math, science, and foreign languages— regular contact with an instructor is a must. During class, the lesson material is presented by the instructor, and you have an opportunity to ask questions. For some students these once a week class sessions aren't enough, and they find themselves overwhelmed at the volume of material presented in a three-hour time span.

The disadvantage of a weekly class schedule is that you must attend class on a regular basis. Instructors find it irritating when students miss class so you must block out time to be there. Frequent classes also means more assignments, more tests, and regular papers.

Weekend Courses

Weekend classes are traditional college classes that are taught on weekends throughout the semester. Some meet every weekend, for example for three hours, every Saturday morning. Others may meet all day Saturday every other week. Weekend classes are aimed at non-traditional college students and older students who work full time and can't fit weekday evening classes into their schedules.

The advantage of a weekend class is that you don't have to attend class after a long day at work. Weekend classes also appeal to students whose workday extends to or starts in the evening and consequently cannot attend evening classes. Another advantage of Saturday classes is the option of attending seven full-day classes rather than fourteen half-day classes. Instead of attending classes every weekend you attend classes every other weekend.

The only disadvantage of weekend classes is that they are held on the weekend. Working parents with young children often complain that they reserve weekend time to spend with their children. Although this is admirable, some time during the weekend probably will have to be sacrificed if you are going to obtain your degree in one year.

Weekend Workshops

Weekend workshops meet for a large block of time on the weekend. Generally, they meet all day Saturday and Sunday for a single credit. Weekend workshops that extend for two or three weekends are worth two or three credits respectively. Instructors often mail weekend workshop students a reading list to be completed before the first class session. A written assignment or take home exam is generally due from one to two weeks after the last class session. Weekend workshops are usually offered in subject areas that can be taught in an activity oriented format. They are also used for courses with a narrow focus such as a seminar on a specific subject area. Disciplines like computer science, physical education, sociology, psychology, and education commonly offer courses in a weekend workshop format.

The main advantage of a weekend workshop is the easy accumulation of credits. Weekend workshops will generally have less written assignments than classes spread over longer periods of time. If you need a credit or two, a weekend workshop is the quickest way to get it. A minor disadvantage of a weekend workshop is they usually are not offered for large amounts of credit. Three credits for a single workshop is rare.

Summer Workshops

Summer workshops are one of the easiest ways to earn three college credits. These workshops meet for extended blocks of time over a one or two week period. A typical one-week schedule is from 8 A.M. to 5 P.M., Monday through Friday. Two-week workshops generally run from 8 A.M. to 12:30 P.M. from Monday to Friday. Both of these schedules meet a total of forty-five hours, the required amount of class time for a three credit course.

Although similar in format, one- or two-week summer workshops are very different. A one-week workshop seldom meets the full forty-five hours, but more typically for thirty to thirty-five hours after allowances are made for lunch, morning and afternoon breaks, late starts, and early dismissals. Homework and tests are minimal or nonexistent. Two-week workshops meet longer since allotments are not made for lunch or early dismissal. Two-week workshops usually have much more homework since students have more time to do it.

Summer workshops can be offered in any subject area that does not require extensive amounts of reading or written homework. Classes like math, science, and history are almost never offered in a one-week format and seldom offered in a two-week format.

Education classes comprise the bulk of summer workshop offerings at most colleges because they're designed to provide inservice training for local teachers. Psychology, art, and computer science may also be included in summer workshop offerings.

Many students worry that summer workshops will be boring because of the extended number of hours involved.

But instructors aware of their inability to keep students en-
tertained vary their teaching style and give several breaks
during the day. A typical day might include a lecture, a movie,
a guest speaker, and several activities. In most workshops
the day goes by very quickly.

Televised Courses

With the advent of cable, closed circuit television, and
VCRs, many colleges use television to teach their introductory level courses. At an initial class session, the professor
explains the schedules for televised class lectures, assignments, and testing. Students are given several options on
when to view pre-recorded video classes. The video classes
are generally broadcast over cable channels and students who
have cable service "attend" class without ever leaving home.
If they find the broadcast schedule inconvenient, students
can tape the classes and replay them later when they have
time. For students without cable service, television classes
are shown during regularly scheduled class time and also
are available at the campus library. Although the content of
the class is taught via television, assignments and tests are
handled in a traditional manner. Students taking televised
classes return to the classroom setting to take exams and to
hand in assignments.

The advantages of televised instruction are numerous.
First, televised instruction is usually more interesting than
traditional classroom instruction. Thousands of dollars have
been spent producing each televised segment. Graphics and
video footage are used to illustrate the principles contained
in the lecture. For instance, a lecture on harp seals doesn't
just talk about the mating behavior of harp seals, it shows
actual footage of their mating. A lecture on probability is
supplemented by graphics and casino gambling footage.
Second, televised instruction saves the time generally wasted
commuting. Since classes can be taped for later viewing,
televised instruction will fit into anyone's schedule. Finally,
video instruction works well for difficult material since you
can replay the parts you don't understand. Students who find

the material difficult after several viewings can call their instructor for assistance.

One major disadvantage of televised instruction is that you lose the benefit of regular interaction with an instructor. Your instructor might be difficult to reach by phone or you might be hesitant to call at home even though you have permission to do so. Televised classes also do not afford you the opportunity to make friends with or receive help from fellow students. A third major problem of televised instruction is that without regularly scheduled classes, it's easy for the undisciplined student to get behind. Some students find themselves three days before the final exam with fifteen or twenty hours of video tapes to watch and learn. Other students complain that watching video tapes is tedious, especially when they're far behind. It's easy to skim a textbook when you're in a jam, but you can't very easily skim a video tape.

Open Learning

Open learning courses provide you with the opportunity to study independently. During an open learning class, students are only required to attend the first and last class sessions. Other classes, if held at all, are optional. During an open learning format course, an instructor guides your learning in optional class seminars by phone and by mail.

During the first class session, the instructor gives the students a detailed syllabus that lists class requirements. It is the student's responsibility to read the assignments, hand in written work on time, study the required material, and take the exams. The instructor may choose to hold occasional optional class meetings, but many do not. It is up to the student to know what to do, how and when to do it.

The advantage of an open learning class is the tremendous time savings and freedom it affords. Time generally wasted commuting back and forth to school or listening to instructors explain material contained in the text book is saved. In an open learning class, you have control of your time, and you can use it as you want.

The disadvantages of an open learning course are that

without regular prodding many students get behind. It is not uncommon for a student to discover two weeks from the end of the semester that there are twenty more chapters to read, three papers to write, and a final exam to take. Another drawback is, if you suddenly find the material difficult, there may be little help available from your professor. A ten-minute phone conversation or a twenty-minute office visit is no substitute for a three-hour class session on a regular basis. For a difficult course, this lack of regular contact with the instructor can pose a serious problem. Open learning classes also rob you of the opportunity of discussing ideas with your fellow students. If working with your fellow students is important to you, you probably won't enjoy classes taught in the open learning format.

High Credit Courses

"High-credit" courses are courses that award more than the conventional three hours of credit per semester. Five- and six-credit classes are high-credit classes. High-credit classes afford the student the opportunity for a quick accumulation of credit. Three six-credit classes, making an eighteen-credit load, is easier to handle than four three-credit classes, which is only a twelve-credit load.

A "credit bargain" is a high-credit class that has the normal number or less than the typically required number of class hours. Normally, a three-credit course meets three hours a week. For example, a studio art class that meets six hours a week for just three hours of credit is not a credit bargain. A biology class that meets three hours a week for lecture and four hours a week for lab, totalling seven class hours a week for five credits is also no credit bargain, while a history class that meets the usual three hours a week but awards four credits is a credit bargain. And, a business course that meets three hours a week yet awards six credits is a super credit bargain.

A smart student looks for high-credit classes that are also credit bargains. If the school you are attending has high-credit classes, sign up for them. A six-credit class is only slightly more work than one three-credit class, but not nearly as much work as two three-credit classes.

Correspondence Courses

Almost one hundred colleges and universities offer correspondence or home study courses. The credits earned through these home study course can be transferred to almost any college in the United States. Most colleges and universities limit the number of correspondence classes you can apply toward your degree. However, there are several schools, including the University of the State of New York and Western Illinois University, that allow you to earn your entire degree via correspondence courses.

These courses are available in hundreds of subjects. You enroll by mail, and the host institution mails your textbook, workbook, assignments, and due dates. Examinations, when required, are either given on the honor system or under the direction of a proctor (a local high school teacher or college professor). Most schools limit how quickly or how slowly you can finish a correspondence class. But the time limits are generous and any serious student can easily finish within them.

Correspondence classes afford students an opportunity for a quick accumulation of credits. Although most schools that offer correspondence courses limit the number of classes you can take at one time, you can take several classes at several different institutions if you really want to accumulate classes very quickly. Correspondence classes offer clear guidelines on what needs to be done to earn credit. The assignments generally are not difficult, since students are expected to progress without the benefit of formal instruction.

The disadvantage of correspondence classes is that many students who enroll in them do not complete them. Without the benefit of regular class meetings, an undisciplined student may not be able to complete the assigned work on time.

Summer School

If you're going to get your degree in one year, summer school is a must. College summer school usually starts a week after spring graduation. Several sessions run back to back with the last session generally ending the same week as the start of the fall semester. Summer sessions can last anywhere from four to eight weeks. The number of hours a single class meets per week varies, depending on the length of the summer session. A general rule is the shorter the summer session, the more frequently classes meet. Classes can meet once, twice, three, or even four times a week. Because of the great number of summer sessions offered and the flexibility of scheduling, it's easy to earn a lot of credits in a short time.

Summer school is more intense than school during fall and spring terms because of the fast pace and compressed class schedule. Some students choose easy courses during the summer, because they don't want to be pressured by the fast pace. Students often shy away from math classes during summer school, because they think that if the classes meet two or three times a week, they won't have enough time to do the assigned homework and fully integrate the material. Other students opt to take difficult courses during the summer because the atmosphere is more relaxed. Summer school classes are smaller, the instructors don't push as hard, and seldom cover as much content as they do during the regular school year.

Other Schools

If you don't find the classes you want at the college or university you are attending, you might have other options. You might be able to take classes at another local school and transfer the credits to the school you are enrolled in as a degree student. Colleges will generally give you permission to take a course from another local college if it's one they don't offer, but they won't give you permission to take a course offered at another college just because it's easier or cheaper. If you want to take classes at another college, get permission to take them before you sign up for them. Many students take courses at another college only to find the credits are not accepted for transfer. To avoid this problem, get permission first, and get it in writing.

Many colleges belong to a consortium of schools. A consortium allows you to take courses at member colleges as though they were your home college.

Resources

Picking the Easiest, Highest Grade-Producing, Least Time-Consuming; Working With Your Advisor and Relating Curriculum Program to Degree Considerations

Cahn, Victor I. *A Thinking Student's Guide to College*. Chris Mass, 1988.

The College Selection Workbook. Beckham House, 1987.

Eaton, Judith *Colleges of Choice*. American Council on Education, 1987.

Hannan, Nancy H. *Going to College*. Albert House Publishers, 1983.

Miller, Gordon P. *Choosing a College*. College Board, 1990.

Roes, Nicholas A. *America's Lowest Cost Colleges*, 6th rev. ed. NAR Productions, 1989.

Sowell, Thomas *Choosing a College* Harper & Row, 1989.

CHAPTER 9
CRITICAL COLLEGE
CRITIQUE

No matter where you live, there is probably more than one college nearby from which you could earn your college degree. Selecting the right college isn't a matter of picking the cheapest, closest, easiest, or most prestigious. A lot of factors should be considered before choosing a school, since the right choice could save you years of time and thousands of dollars.

Knowing something about schools and how they are organized is essential to making the right choice. All schools are not the same. There are colleges, universities, and junior colleges. Even schools of the same type don't organize the school year in the same way. There is not even a uniform grading system among the various colleges and universities around the country.

Junior colleges, community colleges, colleges, and universities are all different types of institutions of higher education. Junior colleges are two-year colleges. Colleges and universities both offer four-year degrees. Traditionally, a college is a subdivision of a university. For example, Harvard University is comprised of several colleges, including liberal arts and sciences, Harvard Business School, Harvard Law School, Harvard Medical School, and Harvard School of Education. Wellesly College, a highly prestigious school for women, offers an undergraduate degree in liberal arts. In the United States, the words college and university are used interchangeably, since many schools, which should really be classified as colleges, call themselves universities to give an impression of greater size and status.

Colleges organize their degree programs around a variety of calendars. The most popular calendar is the **Semester Plan**. The school year is divided into two semesters, the first generally starts on Labor Day and lasts until the week before Christmas. The second semester usually starts in mid-January and ends in mid-May. A course that meets three hours a week for a semester will be worth three semester hours credit. **The Quarter Plan,** in which the entire year is divided into four quarters of equal length, is the second most popular plan. Each quarter is eleven or twelve weeks long. A course that meets for four hours a week for a quarter is worth four quarter hours. In addition to the semester and the quarter plan, there are other calendars. Some schools divide their year into three trimesters. A few schools divide the year into twelve one-month sessions. Students take just one course a month.

Grading systems differ from school to school. **Letter Grades** are the most popular grading system, with *A* being the highest grade and *E* or *F* being the lowest. Some schools give pluses and minuses, others award straight grades. Another popular grading system is the **Pass-Fail System** in which a student is simply awarded a grade of *pass* or *fail*. Some schools allow students to take all their courses on a pass-fail basis, other schools only let students take a limited number of credits pass-fail, generally electives, while many do not allow students to take any course pass-fail. **Number Grades** are a third popular grading system. Students are awarded a grade from 0 to 4. More precise than letter grades, number grades allow professors the option of varying a grade up to one decimal point. For example, a student may receive a grade of 3.2 or 1.6. **Percentage Grades,** popular in the European grading system, give students precise number grades from 0 to 100. Generally 90 to 100 is considered the equivalent of an *A*; 80 to 90 is the equivalent of a *B*; 70 to 79 is equivalent to a *C*; and 60 to 69 is equivalent to a *D*.

In order to help you select the college that is best suited

for you, a simple College Evaluation Form was developed. This five -page form is made up of these six categories:

1. ADMISSION REQUIREMENTS: Since it is useless, time consuming, and expensive to apply to a school where you have no chance of being accepted, this section of the evaluation form will help you to assess your chances of admission.

2. SPEED: Speed is central to an accelerated degree program. This section of the evaluation form will help you to see how quickly you could get your degree from a selected college by determining whether the college has the programs in place that will allow you to get your degree quickly.

3. PROGRAM FLEXIBILITY: The more flexible a program, the easier it will be to get your degree. This section of the form will assist you in evaluating the flexibility of different colleges.

4. COST: The cost of college might be your only reason for choosing one school over another. But the school with the lowest tuition isn't always the cheapest. After you fill out this section, you will have a much better idea of the total bill for a degree at each school you are considering.

5. COURSE SCHEDULING: Students who work need flexible course offerings. In order to match your daily schedule of work, home, and class, it is important that the colleges you are considering offer class formats that meet your particular needs, including evening, weekend, open learning, and even television courses. This section of the evaluation form will help you see if a college has enough course flexibility to match your limited free time.

6. CONVENIENCE FACTORS: Convenience factors, such as computers for student use at the college, although not central to your decision, should be considered carefully when all other factors between colleges are pretty much equal. When time is short, and it will be, and when work and home pressures are excessive, liberal school library hours, student access to computer facilities, and even parking availability can all make your student life easier.

In order to make an educated decision, carefully complete an evaluation for each college choice. Three copies of the College Evaluation Forms are included. If you really want to pick the right college that best matches your needs, don't just look over the forms or partially fill them in. Making a careful college selection is the first and most critical decision you will make toward achieving your degree in one year. Make it wisely.

To fill out the College Evaluation Form, you need to have the catalog and schedule of courses from each college. The information in the catalog and course schedule are kept up-to-date and accurate by the college because these two documents represent the written contract between the school and the students. You can call the college admissions office for a catalog, a schedule of courses, and other admission information including registration forms, tuition assistance forms, in-state tuition forms, and counseling information. They will be happy to send you these documents free of charge. The admissions office personnel are usually very happy to answer your questions or to refer you to the appropriate college office.

COLLEGE EVALUATION FORM

NAME OF COLLEGE: _____

ADDRESS: _____

_____

_____

TELEPHONE: _____

I. ADMISSION REQUIREMENTS

1. a) High School Grade Point Average:

   Minimum GPA Acceptable   My H.S. GPA

   _____   _____

   [To figure your GPA, first multiply the number of
   credits earned by the letter grade factor
     A = 4, B = 3, C = 2, D = 1
   Add these numbers and divide by the total number of
   credits you earned. Round to one decimal point.]

   COLUMN A   COLUMN B
   Credits of A _____ x 4 = _____
   Credits of B _____ x 3 = _____
   Credits of C _____ x 2 = _____
   Credits of D _____ x 1 = _____

   TOTAL   _____   _____
   COLUMN B Total   ___   divided by
   COLUMN A Total   ___   = GPA ___.

b) College required GPA vs. my high school GPA:

   Easily Acceptable (2 tenths over min.) _____
   Barely Acceptable (1 tenth over min.) _____
   Almost Acceptable (1 tenth under min.) _____
   Clearly Unacceptable (2 tenths under min.) _____

2. a) Grade Point Average for Transfer Students:

   Minimum GPA Acceptable My College GPA

   _____   _____

b) College required GPA vs. my high school GPA:
    Easily Acceptable (2 tenths over min.) _____
    Barely Acceptable (1 tenth over min.) _____
    Almost Acceptable (1 tenth under min.) _____
    Clearly Unacceptable (2 tenths under min.) _____

3. a) SAT (Scholastic Aptitude Test) scores:
    College Minimum Acceptable   My SAT Scores
      MATH _____   _____
      VERBAL _____   _____
      COMBINED _____   _____

    (If a college doesn't give their minimum acceptable SAT score, use the published SAT scores for the college.)

b) College required (combined) SAT vs. my SAT:
    Easily Acceptable (100 pts. over min.) _____
    Barely Acceptable (Up to 100 pts. over min.) _____
    Almost Acceptable (Within 100 pts. under min.) ____
    Clearly Unacceptable (More than 100 under min.) __

4. Other Admissions Requirements?   YES ____ NO ____

5. Other Factors to Consider if Needed:

_____

_____

_____

_____

_____

_____

6. Admission Probability:
    Excellent (exceed both GPA & SAT min.) _____
    Good   (exceed one min.; meet one min.) _____
    Fair   (exceed GPA; below SAT min.) _____
    Poor   (meet neither GPA nor SAT) _____

7. a) Is non-degree status an option?   YES _____
                                     NO _____
      b) Is probationary status an option?   YES _____
                                     NO _____

COLLEGE EVALUATION FORM

NAME OF COLLEGE: _____
ADDRESS: _____
_____
_____

TELEPHONE: _____

I. ADMISSION REQUIREMENTS
1. a) High School Grade Point Average:
    Minimum GPA Acceptable   My H.S. GPA

_____ _____

[To figure your GPA, first multiply the number of credits earned by the letter grade factor
    A = 4, B = 3, C = 2, D = 1
Add these numbers and divide by the total number of credits you earned. Round to one decimal point.]

COLUMN A   COLUMN B
Credits of A _____ x 4 = _____
Credits of B _____ x 3 = _____
Credits of C _____ x 2 = _____
Credits of D _____ x 1 = _____

TOTAL _____   _____
COLUMN B Total ____ divided by
COLUMN A Total ____ = GPA ____.

b) College required GPA vs. my high school GPA:

Easily Acceptable (2 tenths over min.) _____
Barely Acceptable (1 tenth over min.) _____
Almost Acceptable (1 tenth under min.) _____
Clearly Unacceptable (2 tenths under min.) _____

2. a) Grade Point Average for Transfer Students:
    Minimum GPA Acceptable My College GPA

_____ _____

b) College required GPA vs. my high school GPA:

Easily Acceptable (2 tenths over min.) _____

Barely Acceptable (1 tenth over min.) _____

Almost Acceptable (1 tenth under min.) _____

Clearly Unacceptable (2 tenths under min.) _____

3. a) SAT (Scholastic Aptitude Test) scores:

College Minimum Acceptable	My SAT Scores
MATH _____	_____
VERBAL _____	_____
COMBINED _____	_____

(If a college doesn't give their minimum acceptable SAT score, use the published SAT scores for the college.)

b) College required (combined) SAT vs. my SAT:

Easily Acceptable (100 pts. over min.) _____

Barely Acceptable (Up to 100 pts. over min.) _____

Almost Acceptable (Within 100 pts. under min.) _____

Clearly Unacceptable (More than 100 under min.) __

4. Other Admissions Requirements? YES ____ NO ____

5. Other Factors to Consider if Needed:

_____

_____

_____

_____

_____

_____

6. Admission Probability:

Excellent (exceed both GPA & SAT min.) _____

Good   (exceed one min.; meet one min.) _____

Fair   (exceed GPA; below SAT min.) _____

Poor   (meet neither GPA nor SAT) _____

7.   a) Is non-degree status an option?   YES _____
                                             NO _____

     b) Is probationary status an option?   YES _____
                                             NO _____

COLLEGE EVALUATION FORM

NAME OF COLLEGE: _____

ADDRESS: _____

_____

_____

TELEPHONE: _____

I. ADMISSION REQUIREMENTS

1. a) High School Grade Point Average:

Minimum GPA Acceptable   My H.S. GPA

_____   _____

[To figure your GPA, first multiply the number of credits earned by the letter grade factor

A = 4, B = 3, C = 2, D = 1

Add these numbers and divide by the total number of credits you earned. Round to one decimal point.]

COLUMN A   COLUMN B

Credits of A _____ x 4 = _____

Credits of B _____ x 3 = _____

Credits of C _____ x 2 = _____

Credits of D _____ x 1 = _____

TOTAL _____   _____

COLUMN B Total _____ divided by

COLUMN A Total _____ = GPA _____.

b) College required GPA vs. my high school GPA:

Easily Acceptable (2 tenths over min.) _____

Barely Acceptable (1 tenth over min.) _____

Almost Acceptable (1 tenth under min.) _____

Clearly Unacceptable (2 tenths under min.) _____

2. a) Grade Point Average for Transfer Students:

Minimum GPA Acceptable   My College GPA

_____   _____

b) College required GPA vs. my high school GPA:
   Easily Acceptable (2 tenths over min.) _____
   Barely Acceptable (1 tenth over min.) _____
   Almost Acceptable (1 tenth under min.) _____
   Clearly Unacceptable (2 tenths under min.) _____

3. a) SAT (Scholastic Aptitude Test) scores:
   College Minimum Acceptable   My SAT Scores
      MATH _____   _____
      VERBAL _____   _____
      COMBINED _____   _____
   (If a college doesn't give their minimum acceptable
SAT score, use the published SAT scores for the college.)

b) College required (combined) SAT vs. my SAT:
   Easily Acceptable (100 pts. over min.) _____
   Barely Acceptable (Up to 100 pts. over min.) _____
   Almost Acceptable (Within 100 pts. under min.) ___
   Clearly Unacceptable (More than 100 under min.) ___

4. Other Admissions Requirements?   YES ___ NO ___

5. Other Factors to Consider if Needed:
_____
_____
_____
_____
_____
_____

6. Admission Probability:
   Excellent (exceed both GPA & SAT min.) _____
   Good   (exceed one min.; meet one min.) _____
   Fair   (exceed GPA; below SAT min.) _____
   Poor   (meet neither GPA nor SAT) _____

7.   a) Is non-degree status an option?   **YES** _____
                                            NO _____
     b) Is probationary status an option?   **YES** _____
                                            NO _____

II. SPEED
1. Life Experience Credits—Max. credits allowed: _____
2. Credit by Exam—Max. credits allowed: _____
3. Cooperative Education—Max. credits allowed: _____
4. Independent Study—Max. credits allowed: _____
5. Credits to Transfer—Max. credits allowed: _____
TOTAL QUICK CREDITS (ADD 1 THROUGH 5) _____

III. PROGRAM FLEXIBILITY

1. Core Requirements # Credits How Specific

English	_____	Very/Somewhat/Not at All
Math/Science	_____	Very/Somewhat/Not at All
Social Science	_____	Very/Somewhat/Not at All
Foreign Language	_____	Very/Somewhat/Not at All
Other	_____	Very/Somewhat/Not at All

2. Req'ments in Major   No. Credits Specific Courses
   Major: _____   _____   _____
                               _____
                               _____
                               _____

3. Req'ments in Minor   No. Credits Specific Courses
   Major: _____   _____   _____
                               _____
                               _____
                               _____

4. Electives Allowed   No. Credits
   Add 1 - 3   _____
   Subtract from 120 _____

IV. COST
1. Life Experience Credits
      Cost per credit x max. credits allowed $ _____
2. Examination Credits
      Cost per credit x max. credits allowed $ _____
3. Tuition
      Cost per credit x max. credits allowed $ _____

4. Books
       Cost per credit x max. credits allowed $ _____

TOTAL COST: ADD 1 - 4 $ _____

V. CLASS SCHEDULING

	Many	Some	Few	None
1. Evening Classes	___	___	___	___
2. Weekend Classes	___	___	___	___
3. Televised Classes	___	___	___	___
4. Open Learning Classes	___	___	___	___
5. Other Schedule Options	___	___	___	___

VI. CONVENIENCE FACTORS

1. Commuting time:

Excellent	(under 15 minutes)	___
Good	(15-30 min.)	___
Fair	(30-45 min.)	___
Poor	(over 45 min.)	___

2. Parking Availability:

Excellent	(free & under 5 min. walk)	___
Good	(free & under 10 min. walk)	___
Fair	(charge or 10 min. walk)	___
Poor	(over 15 min. walk)	___

3. Computer Facilities

	Excellent	Good	Fair	Poor
Availability	___	___	___	___
Software Programs	___	___	___	___

	Excellent	Good	Fair	Poor
Equipment	___	___	___	___
Assistance	___	___	___	___
Waiting Time	___	___	___	___
Hours Open	___	___	___	___

4. Library Hours

	Excellent	Good	Fair	Poor
	___	___	___	___

5. Food Service

	Excellent	Good	Fair	Poor
	___	___	___	___

6. Academic Advising

	Excellent	Good	Fair	Poor
Hours for Appointments	___	___	___	___
Availability via Phone	___	___	___	___

I. ADMISSION REQUIREMENTS

Most colleges decide which students to accept based on a combination of their high school grades, SAT test scores, and letters of recommendation. To assess your chances of being accepted by the schools on your list, fill out Section I of the College Evaluation Form. Take time to compute your high school GPA as well as your GPA for any college courses you have taken. Answer the questions by comparing the admission requirements found in the college catalog with your own high school and college transcripts and test scores. If you don't know what your SAT scores are, you can write to the **College Entrance Examination Board, Box 886, New York, NY 10101-0866.** You will need to identify yourself test by your name and Social Security Number. Include the date and place where you took the examination if you remember.

Question 1. If you have no college transcript, you need to compare your high school grade point average for grades 9, 10, 11, and 12 to the grade point average each college requires for admission that is usually published in the college catalog. If you don't find the minimum high-school GPA listed in the course catalog, call the admissions office.

Decide if your high-school GPA is "*easily acceptable*," more than two decimal points above the minimum; "*barely acceptable*," just one or two decimal points over the minimum; "*almost acceptable*," below the minimum by less than two decimal points; or "*clearly unacceptable*," more than two decimal points under the minimum.

For example, if a college requires a high-school GPA of 3.0 for admission, a GPA of 2.5 is "clearly unacceptable." A GPA of 2.8 or 2.9 is "almost acceptable." A GPA of 3.0 or 3.1 is "barely acceptable." A GPA of 3.3 or higher would be rated as "easily acceptable."

Question 2. If you do have some college credits, you might have to apply as a transfer student. To find out whether this applies to you, look in the college catalog to see how the college defines a transfer student. It could be that if your college credits are over five years old, the college will treat you as a newly entering student. Usually you need at least thirty earned college credits to qualify for transfer student status. If you qualify, compare your college GPA to the minimum GPA required for admission or to the average GPA at the college.

Decide, using the same criteria given for evaluating your high-school GPA, whether your college GPA is "*easily acceptable*," more than two decimal points above the minimum; "*barely acceptable*," just one or two decimal points over the minimum; "*almost acceptable*," below the minimum by less than two decimal points; or "*clearly unacceptable*," more than two decimal points under the minimum.

Question 3. Compare your test scores to the minimum test scores for admission. If minimum SAT scores are not given in the catalog, call the admissions office. If they cannot give you the minimum scores, and many schools don't like to give out this information, ask for the school's average SAT scores. Be sure to ask whether the scores are for traditional students or for adult learners.

Compare your scores and the college minimums or the college average scores. If the college requires a combined SAT score of 1000, a score of 800 would be "*clearly unacceptable*." A combined SAT score of 900 or above would be considered "*almost acceptable*," a combined score between 1000 and 1100 would be "*barely acceptable*," and a combined score over 1100 would be considered "*easily acceptable*."

Question 4. Look in the college catalog to find out whether there are other special admission requirements. If so, list them. Decide if they apply to you, and if you meet them. Mark "YES" or "NO" on the form.

Question 5. List any factors or unusual circumstances that might help you gain admission into a college that normally would not accept you. Some colleges give admission preference to certain minorities such as native Americans. In addition, list any reasons your high school grades or previous college transcript may be less than excellent. Colleges do and will listen to extenuating circumstances. If one of your parents dies during your first year of college, if you had to work to help support yourself or your family, or if your brother or sister were critically injured in an accident, or you got married, had a baby, and the pressures of any of these circumstances caused your grades to plummet, a college might listen to your case sympathetically. But if you dropped out of college to follow the Grateful Dead, used drugs, even if you now claim you're clean, or lost interest in college because of the required core courses, a college admissions committee would be less inclined to grant you admission. If this latter situation applies to you, keep your experiences to yourself and try to seek admission as a probationary student in order to prove your academic ability.

Colleges are not cold and uncaring. They are people who are more than willing to give a break to sincere and talented students.

Question 6. Look over your answers to Questions 1 through 5 to decide your admission probability. If you answered "easily acceptable" to Questions 1, 2, and 3, and you meet the admissions requirements outlined in Question 4, you have an **excellent** chance of being admitted. If all of your answers were in the "easily" or "barely acceptable" range, your chance of admission is **good**. If one or two of your answers were in the "almost acceptable" range, your chances of admission are **poor**.

Question 7. From the college catalog, determine if the college will admit students in probationary status or non-degree status. As a probationary student, you would be registered as a degree candidate, but would be required to earn a minimum GPA during your first semester. If you earn the minimum GPA, you would transfer to full degree status. As a non-degree student, the college allows you to take courses with no promise of admission, regardless of your GPA. After one semester of non-degree status, you may apply for admission as a degree candidate.

II. SPEED
Speed is the second most important category on the

Evaluation Form. By answering the questions in this section, you will be able to very accurately determine how quickly you can get your degree from a particular college.

Question 1. Over five hundred colleges and universities nationwide award credits for life experience by faculty assessment of a detailed and documented portfolio. Use the catalog to find out if the college you're considering awards credit for your life experiences. Read the catalog closely because there is no universally agreed upon name for credits awarded for life experience. You may have to ask the admissions office or academic advisor for assistance.

If the college does not award credit for life experience, place a zero in Question 1. If they do evaluate and give credits for life experience, place the maximum number of credits the college will award in the blank. You will be trying to earn the maximum number.

Question 2. Over twenty-five hundred colleges and universities nationwide accept CLEP, ACT/PEP, and the military equivalent, DANTES, credits through examination. If the college you are considering accepts credits earned by examination, place the maximum number of credits allowed on the evaluation form. If the college doesn't participate in a Credit by Examination Program, place a zero on the evaluation form.

Question 3. If the college you are evaluating has a cooperative education program, enter the maximum number of credits that the college will grant for work projects. If the college does not have a cooperative education program, or if their program would not apply to you in your present job, enter zero.

Question 4. If the college you are evaluating awards credits to independent study projects, enter the maximum number of credits the college will grant for independent study. If the college doesn't allow students to register for independent study, enter a zero.

Question 5. This question has three parts: In part *a*, write the maximum number of transfer credits a school will accept. In part *b*, write the number of transferable credits on your transcript. In order to accept transfer credits, most schools require a grade of *C* or better. In part *c*, put the lower number of credits from either 4*a* or 4*b*.

If you have, say, fifty-two credits to transfer, but the school you are evaluating will only accept thirty transfer credits, then enter thirty, the lesser number of credits. If the college will accept up to sixty transfer credits and you have fifty-two credits, but six credits were below a grade of *C*, you should write forty-six for the credits that will transfer. If you don't have any credits to transfer because the college will not accept your courses, such as a theology course from a college affiliated with a particular denomination, or because your grades were below *C*, then enter zero on the form.

Question 6. Add 1, 2, 3, and 4*c* to determine the maximum number of "quick" credits. Quick credits are the ones you have already earned and can transfer, along with the ones you could quickly obtain by examination, through a cooperative education program, or by being credited for your knowledge gained from experience.

III. PROGRAM FLEXIBILITY

The more flexible a program is, the more quickly you can get your degree. A flexible program means more liberal use of CLEP credits, life experience credits, transfer credits, and cooperative education credits. A lot of specific requirements spell doom to the student who wants to get a degree quickly.

Question 1. All colleges require a set number of general education or "core" courses of all students, regardless of their major. These liberal arts courses assure the college that the students who graduate from their program are "well educated." At some colleges, the core requirements are very vague, such as take six credits of English and six credits of Humanities and Social Science. Other schools have more specific core requirements and state in their English core requirements that students must include one course in American Literature and one course in English Literature.

The number of core requirements in each subject area also differs from college to college. One college might require only six credits in a certain subject area such as English and Composition, while another might require twelve to fifteen credits in the same area. Ideally, the college you select should have the fewest and least specific core requirements to assure you the greatest course flexibility.

Enter the number of core requirements in each of the areas listed on the evaluation form. Next, rate the level of specificity for each set of requirements, either *Very, Somewhat*, or *Not at All.*

Question 2. Select the major you would probably pursue if you were to attend the college you're evaluating. Determine the number of credits the college requires in that major as well as the number of specific courses you will need to take. The fewer number of specific credits required, the quicker you can earn your degree.

Question 3. Select the minor you would probably pursue at the college. Determine the number of credits required in the minor and the number of specific courses required. Less is better here, too.

Question 4. Add the number of required credits you have written for Questions 1 through 3. Subtract the total from 120 credits needed for a degree. The difference is the number of elective credits you will be able to apply to your degree. Electives are essential when incorporating transfer credits, life experience credits, and examination credits. The more electives a degree program allows, the easier, and maybe faster, it will be for you to get your degree.

IV. COST

In order to figure how much it will cost to get a degree, some simple calculations are in order. The cost of a degree at one school over another school may be the deciding factor in choosing your college. The cost of your degree will be the total cost of tuition, special fees like library fee, student union dues, late registration, lab fees, and required fees for graduating seniors, examination charges, the charge to enter life experience credits on your transcript, text books, tutors, typing service, and miscellaneous supplies.

Careful and complete calculation is a must because the school with the lowest tuition might not be the least expensive place for you to get your degree. Credits by examination and life experience programs provide huge cost savings, so that the school with the most flexible programs in these areas could turn out to be the least expensive, although it might have the highest tuition.

Question 1. Life experience credit is generally charged on a per credit basis, at the same rate as credits earned through class enrollment. Some schools charge less than the class enrollment credit rate. It is important that you find out how much the college charges for awarded life experience credits and any "add-on" charges they have. Multiply the per credit charge by the maximum number of life experience credits possible.

Question 2. CLEP, ACT/PEP, and other credit by examination programs are the least expensive ways to earn credits. Determine how many exams you intend to take and multiply the number of exams by the cost per exam. You will pay the same for a three-credit exam such as "Freshman English" as you will for a six-credit exam like "Analysis and Interpretation of Literature." Obviously the six-credit exams are the best cost and credit bargains.

Question 3. Estimating tuition costs is more complex. Start with the 120 credits necessary to earn a college degree and subtract the number of transfer credits you already have. Next, subtract the maximum number of life experience credits allowed, and finally, subtract the number of credits you expect to earn by examination. The remaining number is the number of credits you will need to earn through old fashioned, traditional coursework, or through a cooperative education program. Multiply the number of credits you'll have to earn through class registration by the per credit tuition rate to get a relatively accurate estimate of future tuition costs.

For example, if you have 14 transfer credits, you will need an additional 106 credits to get your degree (120 - 14 = 106). Next, if you figured you could earn the maximum of thirty life experience credits, you still need seventy-six credits for a degree (106 - 30 = 76). Then, after looking over the examination subjects offered by CLEP and ACT, you think you could earn thirty-six credits by examination. Now all you need is forty course credits to get your degree (76 - 36 = 40). The college you are evaluating charges one hundred dollars per credit, so you estimate tuition will cost four thousand dollars ($100 x 40 = $4,000).

Question 4. To estimate the cost of books, assume books will cost an average of seventy-five dollars per course. You can figure out the number of courses you will be registering for by dividing the number of course credits you found you needed in Question 3 by three, since most courses are designated as three-credit courses.

Question 5. To estimate the total cost of your college degree, add up Lines 1, 2, 3, and 4. Remember, this is only an estimate. Tuition rates may increase and your program of study may change.

V. COURSE SCHEDULING

Question 1. Night classes are essential for most adult learners. If your degree program does not have evening classes, you will likely have to juggle your work schedule to enable you to attend class. If you were only taking one class a week, an overlap of work hours and class schedule could probably be worked out. But, if you will be taking several classes a week, you will need to arrange your work hours to eliminate schedule conflicts. If your schedule from Monday to Friday cannot be adjusted, weekend college would be an alternative way to attend classes.

If you happen not to work or if you work at night and are free to attend daytime classes, skip this question. On the other hand, if you do work during the day and night classes are an important consideration, use the schedule of classes from the college to match the courses you need with your available time. Look at the courses offered in the degree program you are considering to determine if the number of night and weekend courses you could take toward your degree, including core courses, major and minor course requirements and electives is: *A Lot, Some, A Few,* or *None.*

Question 2. Weekend classes can be of great assistance in enabling you to earn your degree in the least amount of time. There are two types of weekend classes: 1) Semester-long classes that are usually scheduled for three hours on Saturdays or Sundays, and 2) Single weekend courses that are completed in one sixteen-hour weekend. Single weekend courses generally award one credit for each two-day weekend course that lasts all day Saturday and Sunday. A benefit of the single weekend courses is that they may be scheduled so they do not conflict with other classes, job responsibilities, or planned CLEP examination schedules. Tailored for working adults, these classes fill up fast as they do not conflict with traditional work schedules. Closely review the published schedule of courses to find the number of weekend courses that pertain to your degree requirements.

Question 3. Televised classes allow students to view pre-recorded "classes" taught by professors. Students watch the video presentation and study the accompanying text following a course guide. Televised classes are ideal for the student trying to graduate in one year, since they save valuable commuting time, can be recorded on a VCR to watch and rewatch at any convenient time, or can be reviewed at the school's library. Look through the schedule of classes for each college you are evaluating to locate the number of television classes offered and to determine how many you could take toward your degree program.

Question 4. Open learning classes were designed especially for busy adult learners. They don't require attendance with the customary exception of the first class and the final exam. Open learning classes are the next best thing to televised classes because you go to class the first night, study on your own, mail in papers at appropriate times, and show up for exams. To determine the number of available open learning classes you could take, look in all sections of the college catalog as well as in the schedule of classes. The open learning classes change each semester.

Question 5. Add any other scheduling options the college offers from which you could benefit. For example, some schools offer workshops, courses that run from Monday to Friday from 9:00 A.M. to 5:00 P.M. These workshops, similar to single weekend courses, generally carry three credits for one week's attendance. They are uniquely suited for the non-working student or the student with five consecutive days of leave available to attend class.

V. CONVENIENCE FACTORS

Although not central to deciding on a college, convenience factors can save you hours of time and make a difficult year much easier. In order to evaluate a particular college in the category of convenience factors, a field trip to each college you're considering is in order. Drive or use your planned means of transportation to the campus location of your classes. Take note of the commute time, parking, bus, subway costs, commuter student facilities for eating, studying, the student aid facilities such as the computer centers, and the library facilities including their hours of operation.

Question 1. During an accelerated program you may commute back and forth to the campus on a daily basis. Long commutes eat up time that could be used to study or write papers. Figure out the weekly total of commute time for each college. Be sure to compensate for rush hour delays if they will occur.

Question 2. Most colleges have student commuter parking problems. Nothing can drive a commuting student crazy quicker than cruising around the campus in circles desperately looking for a parking space. If you plan on driving to your classes, assess in advance each school's parking situation and incorporate it into your decision about attending a particular college. You may decide to commute by an alternative means.

Question 3. In the 1990s a personal computer is almost essential for every student. If you don't have access to a PC, don't despair; most colleges have student computer centers equipped with advanced technology computer equipment and software for use by registered students. Pay a visit to the computer facility to check out the equipment, the hours of operation, and the available assistance. Many computer centers are open to students twenty-four hours a day. When you visit, see if there is a waiting line to use the computers and the approximate waiting time. Ask the person in charge when the center is the busiest and when you would have the best chance of using a computer without waiting. Find out which word processing software the center uses to see if it is one you already know or one you could learn easily. Some centers allow students to load their own software programs, others strictly forbid the use of outside programs due to the possibility of computer viruses. If you are fortunate enough to have your own PC at home or one available at work or elsewhere, then obviously computer facilities will not be as much of a convenience factor in making your decision about a college.

Question 4. Take a close look at the college library. The size of its book collection is probably sufficient for your study needs, but are the hours it is open convenient to your schedule? It could be very important that the library keep late night and weekend hours to match your work and class schedule.

Question 5. Evaluate the food service offerings. Most colleges are a city within themselves and have full service along with fast food restaurants throughout the campus. Take time to visit these restaurants and quick food shops to find out the cost, the kind of food available, and the hours they are open.

Question 6. Competent and frequent academic advising is something that is central to your success as a college student. Find out the advising policies for each college you are considering. Determine whether advising is conducted in a central advising office similar to a walk-in clinic, or if you are assigned to a specific advisor once you are admitted. Will advisors answer questions over the phone; must you arrange to see an advisor only by appointment; and how long in advance must appointments be scheduled? Are the advisors available by phone at home; are there evening advising hours?

College Comparison

Once you have completed your College Evaluation Form for each college you're considering, it's time to make the final decision of which college you will apply to for admission. A college comparison form is included so that you can summarize the findings from the College Evaluation Forms and make a quick comparison between colleges on the six factors most critical to an accelerated degree program.

The College Evaluation Form and the College Comparison Form were designed to help you in your decision making, but there are no hard and set rules on evaluating a college. Instead, it is up to you, based on your individual needs and preferences, to make the decision you believe will result in your getting your degree.

Although each of the six factors are important, some factors will have more weight than others. You may choose to make your decision solely on cost, or speed, or convenience. Whichever college you decide upon, you will know that you have made an informed decision.

COLLEGE COMPARISON

	COLLEGE		
	#1	#2	#3

I. ADMISSION REQUIREMENTS

Admission Probability   ___   ___   ___
    (Excellent, Good, Fair, or Poor)

Special Admission Status   ___   ___   ___
    (Yes or No)

II. SPEED

Total Number of Quick Credits   ___   ___   ___

III. PROGRAM FLEXIBILITY

Number of Core Requirements   ___   ___   ___
Number of Major Requirements   ___   ___   ___
Number of Minor Requirements   ___   ___   ___
Number of Electives Allowed   ___   ___   ___

IV. COST

Estimated Cost   ___   ___   ___

V. COURSE SCHEDULING
    (Convenience: Very,   ___   ___   ___
    Somewhat, or Inconvenient)

VI. CONVENIENCE FACTORS
    (Excellent, Good, Fair,   ___   ___   ___
    or Poor)

Resources

Picking the Best College for Earning a Degree in One Year

American Council on Education, Center for Adult Learning and Educational Credentials *The Adult Student's Guide to Alternative and External Degree Programs* New York: Macmillan, 1992.

This guide contains descriptions of over three hundred non-traditional degree programs specifically designed for adult learners.

Barron's *Guide to the Best, Most Popular, and Most Exciting Colleges,* 5th ed. Hauppauge, NY: Barron's, 1991.

The "best" means schools with high admission standards; the "most popular" means schools with large enrollments; and the "most exciting" means schools with unconventional academic programs. This comprehensive directory of over 415 selected U.S. colleges and universities organized in alphabetical order contains hundreds of facts about each school including the men-women ratio for both full-time and part-time students; how the college year is set up, i.e., semesters, summer, or quarters, trimesters; the application deadline; size; average admissions test scores; whether admissions tests are required; programs of study; core requirements, if any; special study programs, i.e., student-designed majors, co-op programs, internships, pass/fail options, general studies degree programs, dual majors, work-study program; CLEP and ACT/PEP credit acceptance; transfer information and requirements; student computer facilities and academic services. The *Guide* gives the admissions phone number and contact person for each institution. It has a college comparison chart for you to fill out using the list of suggested college selection factors.

Barron's *Profiles of American Colleges* Hauppauge, NY: Barron's, 1991.

Profiles of American Colleges gives information for U.S. colleges and universities arranged alphabetically within each geographic region by state. It lists all colleges and universities, large or small, public or private. It ranks the competitiveness, and gives information about application deadlines, composition of students, admissions contact, admissions requirements and procedures, major programs of study, degrees offered, special and general course requirements for graduation, and student facilities and services.

Basta, Nicholas *Major Options: The Student's Guide to Linking College Majors and Career Opportunities During and After College* Harper Perennial: New York, 1991.

This is a useful directory for every college graduate to be. It describes the most popular majors of the approximately 450 currently offered major programs in U.S. colleges. It gives a sample of the types of courses you can expect to take for a selected major along with an assessment by students of each major. Each major lists some typical career choices that are based on having a degree in that major. The second section of *Major Options* describes the jobs generally requiring these popular majors. It describes the routine duties for each job or profession together with the skills necessary to perform the functions of the job. It gives the expected salary and forecast of advancement opportunities and potential career growth for the jobs listed.

De Lafayette, Jean M. *How Your Portfolio Can Earn You an Accredited College Degree Without Setting Foot on Campus,* 3rd ed. ACUPAE, 1990.

This guide lists recognized accredited colleges and universities which award credits liberally for life experience, on-the-job experience, experiential learning and other non-collegiate learning. It lists accredited universities with learning information and learning referral centers nationwide. There is a whole section on how to select schools, programs, and advisors.

Hegener, Karen C., Ed. *Who Offers Part-Time Degree Programs?* 2nd ed. Princeton, NJ: Peterson's Guides, 1985.

Who Offers Part-Time Degree Programs? answers that question with an overview of part-time degree opportunities available at more than 2,500 accredited colleges and universities throughout the United States, including daytime, evening, weekend, summer, external degree, undergraduate, and graduate.

Hunter, John H., Ed., *The Independent Study Cata-*

log: NUCEA's Guide to Independent Study through Correspondence Instruction. Princeton, NJ: Peterson's Guides, 1985.

> *The Independent Study Catalog* is the education "wishbook" for people who want to study without the restrictions of regular class attendance. Students can choose from more than 12,000 correspondence courses offered by 72 colleges and universities. Credit and non-credit courses are available at elementary, high school, undergraduate, and graduate levels.

National University C.E.A. *The Independent Study Catalog: The NUCEA Guide to Independent Study Through Correspondence Institutions* 4th ed. Wells, John H. and Ready, Barbara C., Eds. Peterson's Guides for NUCEA. Princeton, NJ: Peterson's, 1989.

> *The Independent Study Catalog* lists each NUCEA member institution's correspondence courses as well as special courses, the number of the correspondence course, and the course level. This guide gives information about admissions to correspondence study courses, enrollment, registration forms, and catalogs. It details how correspondence study is accomplished, the study materials, textbooks, assignments, evaluation of written assignments, examinations, and transfer of correspondence study credits.

Peterson's Guides *All You Need To Choose the College That's Right for You: Four Year Colleges* Princeton, NJ: Peterson's, 1991.

> *Four Year Colleges* provides detailed college admissions information, matches majors with careers, gives in-depth descriptions of colleges with photographs, profiles, and special announcements. Presented in a narrative format, the margins are indexed to topic, the college, location, majors, degrees, and academic programs.

CHAPTER 10
GETTING IT TOGETHER

Now that you understand the **One Year to a College Degree** Program, it's time to plan your program. This chapter will help you get started toward earning your degree in one year. It will help you select a major, select a minor, design a program of study, a timeline, a study schedule, and a "to do" list. If you follow the guidelines in this chapter, you will be well on your way to earning your degree in one year.

Select a Major

Once you've selected a college or university to attend, selecting a major is the next key decision you must make. The choice of a major is an important one and should be made carefully. It will influence potential career selection and advancement as well as how quickly you earn your degree. Your choice of a major should be based on multiple factors.

Career Advancement

If you are enjoying your current line of work and intend to stay in it, select a major that will help you at your job. Pick a major that requires courses that will help you function more effectively at work. Talk to your supervisors and to other co-workers who are moving up in the organization. Ask them about their college major. Ask them what they would select as a major if they were going to school now.

If you are considering a total change of career, then

your current type of employment should not influence your choice of a major.

Career Change

If you are unhappy with your present line of work and know what line of work you would like to pursue, select a major that matches your career objective. If you know you are unhappy in your current line of work, but you are not sure what field you would like to pursue, consult a career counselor or the career guidance center at the college. A career counselor can evaluate your skills and abilities as well as your interests and personality to help you select a career that matches both your ability and interests.

Transfer Credits

The number of transfer credits you have will influence your choice of a major. If you have over sixty credits, it is probably more efficient to pursue the major you started rather than start a new major. If you have less than thirty transferable credits, your past college major should not influence your current selection of a major. Most of the courses you took can be used to fill general education requirements or as electives. If you have between thirty and sixty transferable credits, a careful analysis should be made of the credits you have to the courses required by the various majors.

Major Requirements

All majors do not have the same number of requirements. Some majors may require as few as twenty-one credits, while others may require as many as sixty credits in the major and related courses. As a general rule professional programs, which must satisfy national, state and local certification requirements, have the most requirements and the most specific requirements. For example, elementary education majors are required to fulfill more requirements than an English or history major. Nursing students have more specific requirements than a mathematics major. More requirements and more specific requirements slow down your progress toward a degree.

Graduate School Admission

If you are considering going to graduate school after you get your degree, having the right undergraduate major may help your admission chances. For instance, graduate programs in clinical psychology prefer students with an undergraduate major in psychology. Other graduate school programs may not discriminate in their admission procedures regarding students with inappropriate majors; instead they require students of other majors to make up missed course work. For example, most MBA programs will accept talented students with any undergraduate major but require all students to have at least two semesters of accounting and one semester of calculus. Students without accounting or calculus must take these and/or other required courses, which are not counted toward their degree, prior to admission.

Background and Experience

When selecting a major be sure to consider your background and experience. Relevant experience might help in your coursework. You may also be able to earn life experience credit, which can be applied to your major. For example, if you've worked in the banking industry for the past ten years, you'll find it easier to earn a degree in business than in an area where your background is limited.

Aptitude

Aptitude is important when selecting a major. Look over all the requirements for the major you are considering and decide if you can easily pass all of them. Examine the math requirements carefully. They are a major stumbling block for many students. Some majors require no math at all, while others require at least two semesters of calculus.

Tuition Reimbursement

Your employer may reimburse you for college expenses. Some employers restrict their reimbursement to work related courses, while others will reimburse any college course work. Employers may limit reimbursement to courses in which you earned a minimum grade of *B*. If finances are a major concern, find out if your employer is willing to pay your tuition, and if so, in what areas. If not, you might find it economically beneficial to find a job in an organization that has a college reimbursement program that begins as soon as someone is hired.

Select Your Minor

Once you have selected your major, it's time to select a minor. Several factors will influence your choice of a minor.

Your Major

The number one influence on the selection of a minor is the choice of a major. Certain majors virtually predetermine the student's minor. Biology majors are generally chemistry minors, since so many chemistry courses are required for a biology degree. Physics majors are generally math minors.

Other fields, such as English or history, don't require numerous related courses. Students who major in these areas, generally have a great deal of freedom in selecting a minor.

Transfer Credits

If you decide not to apply your previous transfer credits to your major, you may want to apply them to your minor. Using your transfer credits for either your major, minor, or general education requirements frees up your electives.

Minor Requirements

Minors also vary in the number of courses they require. If you want to get out of school fast, pick a minor with as few requirements as possible.

Personal Interests

A minor is an area of study where you can pick something in which you have a personal interest. If you are interested in a specific subject, you will find it easier and more enjoyable to study.

Background and Experience

Use your background and experience to satisfy the requirements for your minor quickly. Previous background and experience translates into less study time and potential life experience credits. If you are a native speaker of Spanish, you may want to select Spanish as a minor. If you have been working with computers for the past ten years, you could minor in computer science and use your knowledge to your advantage. If you have raised a family, you have inadvertently learned a great deal about child development which could help you in any one of several minors related to childhood development, early childhood, or elementary education.

Aptitude

Pick a minor for which you have a natural aptitude. Everyone doesn't have the same abilities. If you have a natural talent, select a minor in that area. You may be a natural mathematician, a talented artist or musician, or a speed reader. If so, pick a minor that uses your abilities.

When selecting a minor, you should weigh all six of these factors carefully. But since speed and efficiency are major objectives, do not weigh all six factors equally. The first three factors listed: **Major Selected, Transfer Credits,** and **Minor Requirements** should be given the most weight.

Design a Program of Study

Now that you have selected a major and a minor, it's time to design a program of study. A program of study is a plan of your entire degree program. It keeps track of what you've taken and what you need to take. Your program of study is your road map for earning your college degree in one year.

It order to design your program of study sheet, follow the step by step instructions below. If you get confused, study Eileen's program of study, which is located in chapter three.

Step I—List Requirements

Go through the course catalog and write down the core requirements as well as the requirements for the major and minor you have chosen. List these requirements down the left side of **Program of Study—Planning Sheet.**

PROGRAM OF STUDY—PLANNING SHEET

GENERAL ED. REQUIREMENTS (_____ credits)

_____	TR LE EX CO CL	_____
_____	TR LE EX CO CL	_____
_____	TR LE EX CO CL	_____
_____	TR LE EX CO CL	_____
_____	TR LE EX CO CL	_____
_____	TR LE EX CO CL	_____
_____	TR LE EX CO CL	_____
_____	TR LE EX CO CL	_____
_____	TR LE EX CO CL	_____
_____	TR LE EX CO CL	_____
_____	TR LE EX CO CL	_____

MAJOR REQUIREMENTS (_____ credits)

_____	TR LE EX CO CL	_____
_____	TR LE EX CO CL	_____
_____	TR LE EX CO CL	_____
_____	TR LE EX CO CL	_____
_____	TR LE EX CO CL	_____
_____	TR LE EX CO CL	_____
_____	TR LE EX CO CL	_____
_____	TR LE EX CO CL	_____
_____	TR LE EX CO CL	_____
_____	TR LE EX CO CL	_____
_____	TR LE EX CO CL	_____

MINOR REQUIREMENTS (_____ credits)

_____	TR LE EX CO CL	_____
_____	TR LE EX CO CL	_____
_____	TR LE EX CO CL	_____
_____	TR LE EX CO CL	_____
_____	TR LE EX CO CL	_____
_____	TR LE EX CO CL	_____
_____	TR LE EX CO CL	_____
_____	TR LE EX CO CL	_____
_____	TR LE EX CO CL	_____
_____	TR LE EX CO CL	_____

ELECTIVES (_____ credits)

_____	TR LE EX CO CL	_____
_____	TR LE EX CO CL	_____
_____	TR LE EX CO CL	_____
_____	TR LE EX CO CL	_____
_____	TR LE EX CO CL	_____
_____	TR LE EX CO CL	_____
_____	TR LE EX CO CL	_____
_____	TR LE EX CO CL	_____
_____	TR LE EX CO CL	_____

STEP II: List Your Transfer Credits. Use a copy of your college transcripts to list all the transferable college credits. Your transcript lists all the courses you took in chronological order, semester by semester or quarter by quarter. To help with your planning, reorganize your courses by subject. For example, list all math courses together, all English courses together, and all foreign language courses together. All courses with a C (2.0) or better will transfer, so omit courses with a grade of a D or below. List the course number, course name, and the grade you received.

Transfer Credit List

UNIV.	SEM/YR	COURSE NO.	NAME	GRADE
_____	_____	_____	_____	_____
_____	_____	_____	_____	_____
_____	_____	_____	_____	_____
_____	_____	_____	_____	_____
_____	_____	_____	_____	_____
_____	_____	_____	_____	_____
_____	_____	_____	_____	_____
_____	_____	_____	_____	_____
_____	_____	_____	_____	_____
_____	_____	_____	_____	_____
_____	_____	_____	_____	_____
_____	_____	_____	_____	_____
_____	_____	_____	_____	_____
_____	_____	_____	_____	_____

You may be able to earn credit for courses taken at work, in the military, or given by a professional organization. List any courses, seminars, or workshops you took through work or on your own which may be creditable. Remember, you must have official documentation of your enrollment in these courses.

W/SHOP	DATES	CRSE NO.	NAME	GRADE
_____	_____	_____	_____	_____
_____	_____	_____	_____	_____
_____	_____	_____	_____	_____
_____	_____	_____	_____	_____
_____	_____	_____	_____	_____
_____	_____	_____	_____	_____
_____	_____	_____	_____	_____
_____	_____	_____	_____	_____
_____	_____	_____	_____	_____

STEP III: Life Experience Credits. Another way to earn quick credits toward your degree is through life experience. List the life experiences you have that may be creditable. For planning purposes, list your life experience and the parallel course or courses that relate to it.

EXPERIENCE	RELATED COURSE	CREDIT
_____	_____	_____
_____	_____	_____
_____	_____	_____
_____	_____	_____
_____	_____	_____
_____	_____	_____
_____	_____	_____
_____	_____	_____

STEP IV: Exam Credits. You can earn college credit by taking an exam. Here is a list of the examinations offered by the major testing agencies. Look at the list and decide whether OR NOT you think you could pass them. Circle the letters that match your proficiency in each subject area.

W/O = You could probably pass now **without** studying.

SOME = You could probably pass with **some** studying.

A LOT = You could probably pass with **a lot** of studying.

NEVER = You could **never** pass no matter how much you studied.

You will take the examinations marked **Without** or **Some**.

College Level Examination Program (CLEP) Tests

HISTORY AND SOCIAL SCIENCES

	AMT. OF STUDY NEEDED			
American Government	W/O	Some	A Lot	Never
American History I	W/O	Some	A Lot	Never
American History II	W/O	Some	A Lot	Never
Western Civilization I	W/O	Some	A Lot	Never
Western Civilization II	W/O	Some	A Lot	Never
General Psychology	W/O	Some	A Lot	Never
Educational Psychology	W/O	Some	A Lot	Never
Human Growth and Dev.	W/O	Some	A Lot	Never
Introductory Sociology	W/O	Some	A Lot	Never
Introductory Macroeconom	W/O	Some	A Lot	Never
Introductory Microeconom	W/O	Some	A Lot	Never

FOREIGN LANGUAGES

College French—1 & 2	W/O	Some	A Lot	Never
College German—1 & 2	W/O	Some	A Lot	Never
College Spanish—1 & 2	W/O	Some	A Lot	Never

COMPOSITION AND LITERATURE

American Literature	W/O	Some	A Lot	Never
Analysis/Interp. of Lit.	W/O	Some	A Lot	Never
College Composition	W/O	Some	A Lot	Never
English Literature	W/O	Some	A Lot	Never
Freshman English	W/O	Some	A Lot	Never

SCIENCE AND MATHEMATICS

Calculus/Elem Functions	W/O	Some	A Lot	Never
College Algebra	W/O	Some	A Lot	Never
Trigonometry	W/O	Some	A Lot	Never
College Algebra-Trig.	W/O	Some	A Lot	Never

| General Biology | W/O | Some | A Lot | Never |
| General Chemistry | W/O | Some | A Lot | Never |

BUSINESS

Computers and Data Proc	W/O	Some	A Lot	Never
Introduction to Mgmt	W/O	Some	A Lot	Never
Introductory Accounting	W/O	Some	A Lot	Never
Introductory Business Law	W/O	Some	A Lot	Never
Introductory Marketing	W/O	Some	A Lot	Never

List of ACT/PEP Examinations

ARTS AND SCIENCES

Abnormal Psychology	W/O	Some	A Lot	Never
Anatomy and Physiology	W/O	Some	A Lot	Never
Foundations of Gerontol	W/O	Some	A Lot	Never
Microbiology	W/O	Some	A Lot	Never
Physical Geology	W/O	Some	A Lot	Never
Statistics	W/O	Some	A Lot	Never

BUSINESS

Corporation Finance	W/O	Some	A Lot	Never
Introductory Accounting	W/O	Some	A Lot	Never
Principles of Management	W/O	Some	A Lot	Never
Principles of Marketing	W/O	Some	A Lot	Never
Production/Oper. Mgmt.	W/O	Some	A Lot	Never

EDUCATION

Educational Psychology	W/O	Some	A Lot	Never
Reading Instr. in Elem. Sch.	W/O	Some	A Lot	Never
Read. Instr. Theoret. Found.	W/O	Some	A Lot	Never

NURSING

Fundamentals of Nursing	W/O	Some	A Lot	Never
Maternity Nursing	W/O	Some	A Lot	Never
Matern./Child Nursing I&II	W/O	Some	A Lot	Never
Adult Nursing	W/O	Some	A Lot	Never
Psych./Ment. Hlth. Nursing	W/O	Some	A Lot	Never
Com. in Nursing Care I & II	W/O	Some	A Lot	Never
Diff. in Nursing Care I & II	W/O	Some	A Lot	Never
Occupational Strat./Nursing	W/O	Some	A Lot	Never
Professional Strat./Nursing	W/O	Some	A Lot	Never
Health Support I & I	W/O	Some	A Lot	Never

STEP V: Cooperative Education Credits. Now think of a work-related project that you could do in approximately three to four months that relates to one, two, or three courses listed in the course catalog.

Project Description:_____

_____

Courses: _____

_____

STEP VI: Independent Study Credits. Plan on earning a minimum of six independent study credits. Think of a hobby or work-related project that you could complete easily. Briefly describe the project, the department in which the credits would be awarded, and the number of credits that you would request.

Project Title:_____

Project Description:_____

_____

Department:_____

Credit Request: _____

_____

STEP VII: Design a Plan of Action. Now it's time to enter the information from Steps I to VI into the **Program of Study—Planning Sheet.** You may have to juggle the credits you earned and will earn through transfer, examination, life experience, and cooperative education to come up with the best fit for your plan.

1. Match the transfer credits listed in Step I with the courses listed under the categories of *General Education Requirements, Major Requirements,* and *Minor Requirements* of the **Program of Study—Planning Sheet.** Enter the courses in the right hand column of the chart.

2. Circle the letters **TR** for the course requirements you expect to satisfy by transfer credits.

3. Place the name and number of the course along with where you took it at the end of the line.

4. Place any course you want to transfer and count toward your degree, but does not fit under the sections entitled *General Education, Major Requirements,* and *Minor Requirements* in the *Electives* section.

5. Now enter the courses for which you expect to earn life experience credits in the right hand column of the **Program of Study—Planning Sheet.**

6. Circle **LE** for the *General Education, Major,* and *Minor* course requirements you expect to satisfy using **Life Experience Credit**.

7. On the blank space at the end of the line, write a two or three word description of the experience you had.

8. Place any life experiences you expect to get credit for, but which do not fit under *General Education, Major Requirements,* or *Minor Requirements* in the *Electives* section.

9. Now enter the credits you expect to earn by examination with the courses listed on the **Program of Study— Planning Sheet.**

10. Circle **EX** for the *General Education, Major,* and *Minor* course requirements you expect to satisfy by examination.

11. Write the name of the testing organization and the name of the exam on the blank space at the end of the line.

12. Place the names of the examinations you expect to pass and earn credit for under the *Electives* section.

13. If you selected a cooperative education project, assume you will earn six credits. Place these six credits in the appropriate area, *General Education, Major Requirements, Minor Requirements,* or *Electives*. If you do not choose to do a work study project, leave this area blank.

14. If you plan on doing an independent study project, enter these credits in the appropriate area, *General Education, Major Requirements, Minor Requirements* or *Electives*.

15. The course lines that are still blank will be filled by selecting traditional classroom courses. Circle the word *COURSE* on the **PROGRAM OF STUDY—PLANNING SHEET** for each required course that has no other letters circled.

16. Now look through the course catalog and pick courses that match the requirements. On the blank at the right, list all the courses that would fill the requirement. Be sure to list all the options. If you list only one possibility, your

flexibility will be greatly reduced. A course you need might be offered at the same time as another course you need; it might not be offered when you need it; or it may be offered only when you have to work. By increasing your options, you increase your flexibility.

17. Select your electives. You need to consider several things when selecting electives so that your final program of study will be to your best advantage.

a. Consider whether you intend to apply for any specific licensure or certification. If there are some specific courses that are required for licensure or certification, but are not part of your degree requirements, then you might want to take these required courses as electives. For example, teaching requires certification, and although you are not an education major, you might want to choose education courses as electives so you can apply for a teaching certificate at a later date.

b. You could choose electives that will give you a better background for graduate school. Suppose you are an undergraduate mathematics major, but you intend to go to graduate school in computer science. Taking electives in computer science will strengthen your chances of admission into graduate school in computer science and save you time and money once you are admitted.

c. You should also select electives that are easy. Difficult electives take valuable time that is needed to study required courses you find difficult. If you have a strong background in a particular area and you did not earn equivalent credit by examination, select electives from this area of strength.

d. Scheduling is also an important factor to consider when choosing electives. Often you will be prompted to select an elective simply because it fits your schedule for graduating in one year. Of course, looking through the college course schedule and saying, "what is offered on Monday evenings from 7 to 10 P.M.," isn't the best way to select an elective, but it may be necessary.

e. Finally, you may want to select a course based on

your personal interest. For the four-year student, this is primarily the way electives are selected. But for the student intending to graduate in one year, this is not the most important factor to consider.

Designing a Timeline

Now that you know everything you need to do to earn your degree, you have to decide when to do what. Designing a time line can help you make sure you complete your program of earning a degree in one year on time. Prioritizing your activities and picking target dates will help keep you on target.

In order to get things done on time, you're going to have to gather a lot of important information. You'll need to know what courses are offered when, application and registration deadlines for school, standardized tests, and special programs. By finding out all this information ahead of time you can make sure you are not shut out of critical programs and courses.

Here are some key dates you need to know right away:

1. **Application Deadline for Admission to the College of Your Choice** _____

First and foremost you should apply to the college of your choice. Apply for the next possible semester. Start in the spring or summer if that is the closest semester. Don't delay. You've put off going to school long enough. Don't delay any more.

2. **Transcript Evaluation–Preliminary Evaluation Appointment Date** _____

You don't have to be admitted to a college to have your transcript evaluated. Set up an appointment with the admissions office to have your transcript evaluated as soon as possible. An admissions officer will be able to give you a good idea which courses will transfer and what other experiences or courses you have that may be eligible for credit. The admissions officer may also be able to suggest a major that fits your background and experience and will be easy to complete.

3. Life Experience Credits Application Deadline.

Earning life experience credits is a two-step process. First you need to apply to the program and then you have an entire semester to compile your portfolio and document your experience. These credits are critical to completing your degree quickly so you need to apply for these life experience credits as soon as possible.

4. Establish a Semester by Semester Schedule.

Decide what courses you are going to take each semester. There are three semesters listed here, one of them being summer school. If you start in the fall, your three-semester program would be fall, spring, and summer. If you start in the spring, your three semesters would be spring, summer, and fall. If you start school in the summer, your three semesters would be summer, fall, and spring. It doesn't matter when you start, just that you organize your program into three semesters. If you decide after organizing a three-semester plan that the load is too much for you, redesign your plan into four or five semesters.

Semester I—Date _____
Registration Deadline _____
Courses to be Taken   Credits

_____   _____

_____   _____

_____   _____

_____   _____

_____   _____

Credit by Examination (CLEP & PEP)
Exam Title   PEP/CLEP   Date Reg. Date

_____   _____   _____ _____

_____   _____   _____ _____

_____   _____   _____ _____

_____   _____   _____ _____

_____   _____   _____ _____

Semester II—Date _____

Registration Deadline _____

Courses to be Taken   Credits

_____   _____

_____   _____

_____   _____

_____   _____

_____   _____

_____   _____

Credit by Examination   (CLEP & PEP)

Exam Title   PEP/CLEP   Date   Reg. Date

_____   _____   _____   _____

_____   _____   _____   _____

_____   _____   _____   _____

_____   _____   _____   _____

_____   _____   _____   _____

_____   _____   _____   _____

Cooperative Education Project

Title _____ Credits _____

Independent Study Project

Title _____ Credits _____

Semester III—Date _____

Registration Deadline _____

Courses to be Taken   Credits

_____   _____

_____   _____

_____   _____

_____   _____

_____   _____

Credit by Examination   (CLEP & PEP)

Exam Title   PEP/CLEP   Date   Reg. Date

_____   _____   _____   _____

_____   _____   _____   _____

_____   _____   _____   _____

_____   _____   _____   _____

Make a Monthly Calendar

The monthly calendar is where all key dates are written. In an effort to keep track of everything, you don't want to forget to do something important. Here are the main things that should be put on your monthly calendar.

* Assignment due dates
* Exam dates
* CLEP/PEP registration dates
* CLEP/PEP test dates
* Appointments with faculty members or your advisor
* Pre-registration dates

You don't have to buy an expensive calendar. A simple sheet of note book paper will do just fine and give you ample room to write. Here is a sample monthly calendar:

October 1, Tuesday Math Page 40
October 2, Wednesday Read English
October 3, Thursday Math Page 45
October 4, Friday
October 5, Saturday
October 6, Sunday
October 7, Monday Read Psychology
October 8, Tuesday Math Page 52
October 9, Wednesday Read English
October 10, Thursday Math Page 56
October 11, Friday CLEP November Registration
October 12, Saturday CLEP Exams (History 1 & 2)
October 13, Sunday
October 14, Monday Read Psychology
October 15, Tuesday Math Page 63
October 16, Wednesday English Paper #1
October 17, Thursday Math Page 67
October 18, Friday
October 19, Saturday
October 20, Sunday
October 21, Monday Psychology Assignment
October 22, Tuesday Math Exam
October 23, Wednesday Read English

October 24, Thursday
October 25, Friday
October 26, Saturday
October 27, Sunday
October 28, Monday
October 29, Tuesday   Math Page 78, Psych Midterm
October 30, Wednesday Read English
October 31, Thursday Math Page 85

Setting a Weekly Schedule

If you're going to be successful in earning your college degree in one year, you are going to have to organize your time carefully. For the next year you don't have a minute to waste. Planning is the key to efficiency. Disorganization will waste time, your most valuable asset.

Your weekly schedule outlines what you will do hour by hour during the upcoming week. Although a tight schedule is confining, the benefits of careful planning are tremendous.

* With a pre-established schedule, you are more likely to study and less likely to procrastinate.

* A schedule forces you to study the subjects you dislike rather than avoid them because you find them difficult or tedious.

* By keeping you up to date, a schedule eliminates the need for cramming.

* By establishing a regular study schedule, tasks that seem overwhelming are broken down into small parts and are suddenly manageable.

* Scheduling study breaks as well as study time assures that your free time as well as your study time stay a preset length. Extensive breaks are eliminated.

Making a Schedule

An effective schedule will have three components—fixed activities, a weekly schedule, and a daily schedule.

Fixed activities are the activities that you do on a regular basis. Work, class attendance, church, meals, and sleep are all examples of fixed activities. Type up your fixed schedule and make multiple copies of it. On this schedule form, you will add your weekly and daily activities.

Here is a sample fixed schedule:

Mon	Tue	Wed	Thur	Fri	Sat	Sun
6-7		Dress and Breakfast				
7-8		Commute to Work				
8-12		Work				
12-1		Lunch				
1-5		Work				
5-6		Commute Home				
7-8						
8-9						
9-10						
10-6		Sleep				

Determine your weekly schedule. There are two parts to making a weekly schedule. Every Sunday night make a list of all the things you need to accomplish during the week. For example, if you need to write a paper, study for a test, read your history assignment, do your math homework, or call your advisor, put these items on your weekly activities list. Next to each task write how much time you think it will take. Once the list is complete, place these items on your fixed schedule.

Making a "To Do" List

Every morning you should make a daily *"Things To Do"* list. Your daily "To Do" list would include everything on the weekly schedule for that day, as well as items that you didn't know about Sunday night, but that come up on a daily basis: a new assignment you just found out about that is due in two days, a letter telling you that you need to meet with your advisor as soon as possible, a store you have to go to, an emergency requiring tires for the car. Next to each item on the list put how long you estimate it will take to accomplish. Next, prioritize the items on the list. Put *As* next to the things that are the most important and must be done right away, *Bs* next to the items that are less important and can wait a while, and Cs next to the least important items, which can wait indefinitely. Everything you want to get accomplished should be on your "To Do" list. As you complete an item, cross it off your list.

Here is a sample "To Do" list:

C   Call the tire store for an appointment.

A   Go to clinic to get eyes examined at 2 P.M.

C   Get books from the library for paper due in two weeks.

B   Read chapter of biology.

A   Do math homework.

A   Study history notes for test.

B   Listen to Spanish tape.

C   Wash and clean out the car.

The reason most people don't manage their time well is because they tend to do the easiest rather than the most important jobs first. It is easier to call for an appointment to have the car serviced or stop by the library rather than study for a test or do a difficult math homework assignment. A carefully prioritized "To Do" list helps you overcome these problems and get things done on time.

Overcoming Procrastination

Students often procrastinate on a large assignment because they don't know how to get started. The twenty-five-page psychology paper that counts 80 percent of your grade seems overwhelming. Students also procrastinate on tasks that seem difficult. To overcome either of these problems, break down a difficult or overwhelming task into a list of smaller, easier tasks.

For example, that twenty-five-page psychology paper on the stresses mothers experience when returning to work can be broken down into a number of smaller steps. These smaller steps are easier and less frightening.

a. Go to library and get books on returning to work.

b. Write interview questions to interview women who recently returned to work after a long absence.

c. Read books from library.

d. Outline paper.

e. Show outline and questionnaire to instructor.
f. Start list of names of women who recently returned to work and are eligible to interview.
g. Start writing.
h. Edit draft of paper.

Although the entire task seems overwhelming, going to the library or writing the questionnaire is not. Once these first tasks are complete, the pump is primed, and most students can progress on their own. If you're still having trouble, ask your instructor for help.

Finding and Using Small Amounts of Time

For the working student every spare minute of time is a valuable asset. In order to work and earn your college degree in one year, you must squeeze every spare minute of time out of your schedule. Things that you once considered essential must be eliminated from your schedule. Reading the newspaper, watching television, idly listening to music, playing computer games, having lunch with colleagues and friends, although enjoyable take valuable time that could be used more productively.

Here are small amounts of time you probably waste that you could use more efficiently.

Commuting to Work—The average American commutes forty-five minutes each way to work, that's an hour and a half a day, or seven and a half hours a week.

Commuting to Class—Commuting thirty minutes each way to school is typical. If you attend five classes per week, that's five valuable hours a week.

Lunchtime—Most people take a full hour for lunch but could easily eat in only fifteen minutes. Save forty-five minutes a day or three hours and forty-five minutes a week by bringing your lunch to work.

In the Car—Many people spend an additional ten hours a week in the car, driving to the grocery store, running errands, driving to/from entertainment, driving carpools. Consolidating trips will reduce the time spent in the car. Arranging for or paying others to do the errands or drive the carpools would give you back precious time.

Waiting—This is a hurry up and wait society. Be sure to be at the doctor's by three, then sit and wait for a half hour. Wait for a meeting to begin; wait in the check out line of the grocery store; everywhere you go you wait. Reclaiming this one hour of wait time per day adds an additional seven hours of study time a week to your schedule.

By reclaiming the time you generally waste commuting, in the car, at lunch, waiting, and doing other non-essential, non-productive activities, you could easily find over thirty hours a week to study. In order to use these not so little bits of time more effectively, you need to prepare in advance. Here are two tips that can reduce your extra study time to almost zero.

First, when you read, take notes on large index cards (4x6). Index cards fit readily into your pocket, contain small amounts of information that can be studied easily, and can be looked at anywhere. *Next, make a second set of notes on a cassette tape.* These notes should be a list of key concepts, facts, and vocabulary. Play these tapes while commuting, waiting, or running errands. These two tools, your note cards and your cassette tapes, will help you utilize the thirty hours a week you normally waste. Here are some ways to use these key techniques most effectively:

Commuting to Work—If you take the subway, bus, or carpool to work, you could read assigned work. If you can't read, study pre-written notes or listen to note tapes using earphones on a portable tape player. If you drive to work and reading is impossible, listen to a tape of class lectures in the car's cassette player. If you don't tape your instructor's lectures, make your own study tapes and listen to them. Make tapes while you are reading the assignments; record key facts and terms.

Commuting to Class—If you take public transportation to school, use this time to read or listen to tapes. If you drive, listen to tapes in your car. If your car doesn't have a tape deck, you can buy an adapter so that you can plug your regular tape recorder into the cigarette lighter. You could also get a speaker for your portable cassette player.

Lunch Time—The extra time you save at lunch can be

a big help. If you use it to do things you have to do anyway, the *As* on your daily "To Do" list, you will free up a big block of time in the evening. You can use it to make required phone calls, pay bills, outline a paper, work on a homework assignment, take notes, read, or study.

Waiting—To get the best use out of your waiting time, carry a textbook, index cards, or xerox copy of a chapter with you at all times. Reading small snatches of material here and there adds up quickly.

In the car—Whenever you are in the car, whether driving or riding, whether you're alone or have company, listen to your homemade or professionally made class-related tapes.

Resources

Study Guides and Student Aids

Bianchi, Anne *Smart Choices: A Woman's Guide to Returning to School*. Princeton, NJ: Peterson's Guides, 1990.

> Discusses problems of returning women students trying to blend academic life and her "other" lives. Has no-nonsense advise presented in a friend-to-friend style for any woman contemplating returning to college.

Fry, Ronald *How to Study: The Comprehensive Guide for Students* New York: The Career Press, 1991.

> *How To Study* is one of a series of five student study aid books. Its list of chapters quickly describes the contents: "How to Start Out Right," How to Organize Your Studying," How To Read and Remember," How to Organize Your Time," How to Excel in Class," How to Use Your Library," How to Write Better Papers," and "How to Study for Tests." *How To Study* includes much useful advice along with some exercises to help you incorporate the new study aids into your study habits. This isn't a book to read, its a book to use. Every student will find some new ideas in it that will make studying easier.

Fry, Ronald *How To Take Notes: The Comprehensive Guide for Students*. New York: The Career Press, 1991.

Another in the series of five *How To* student study aid books. *How To Take Notes* gives new and seasoned students from high school through graduate school information about what is worth taking notes on, how to capture the important information from oral lectures, and from printed material in texts and research documents. It includes directions on note-taking equipment, gives guidance on learning to listen, strategies for taking class notes, using note taking shorthand, making notes of chapters, library materials and making notes for use in oral reports. Complete with examples, *How to Take Notes* is a helpful aid for any student.

Fry, Ronald *How To Manage Your Time: The Comprehensive Guide for Students* New York: The Career Press, 1991.

How To Manage Your Time is another small book in the series. It describes in simple language the key factors in successful time management planning. Complete with charts and worksheets, it can help any student learn the basics of time management without taking much time to do so.

Galica, Gregory S.*The Blue Book: A Student's Guide to Essay Exams* San Diego: Harcourt Brace Jovanovich, 1991.

You may be required to take essay exams when earning credit by examination; and you will definitely be required to take essay exams during traditional coursework. Written by a college professor, this little guide can be a life saver. It gives strategies for studying and taking essay examinations and provides tips on how to choose which exam questions to answer, decide how long an essay to write, and how to organize an answer. It provides strategies for answering the most common types of essays: complex fact essays, opinion essays, compare and contrast essays.

Jensen, Eric *Student Success Secrets* New York: Barron's, 1982.

Written in large, easy to read print, with plenty of illustrations, *Student Success Secrets* contains a narrative description of success strategies followed by examples, step by step directions, and techniques. Each chapter has an end review table of each point that was covered in the chapter. These end-chapter reviews are good reminders to keep handy to look at from time to time.

Turkel, Judi Kesselman and Peterson, Franklynn *Note-Taking Made Easy* Chicago: Contemporary Books Inc., 1982.

Note-Taking Made Easy tells exactly how to determine what's worth noting from lectures, class discussions, readings, meetings. Gives the two most successful methods of organizing notes.

Turkel, Judi Kesselman and Peterson, Franklynn *Test-Taking Strategies* Chicago: Contemporary Books Inc., 1981.

Test-Taking Strategies advises students how to successfully take a wide variety of tests including: multiple choice, true/false, matching questions, verbal analogy, short answer, fill in the blank, vocabulary tests, number problem tests, math or figure series, reading comprehension, essay exams, and oral examinations.

Turkel, Judi Kesselman and Peterson, Franklynn *Study Smarts* Chicago: Contemporary Books Inc., 1981.

Each of *Study Smarts* 16 very short chapters gives a learning "tip." The whole book is short, useful, quick and easy to skim for very practical study advice and techniques.

A Final Note

If you need help selecting a college, planning a program of study, or deciding whether or not to return to college, we can help.

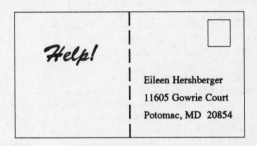

Send a postcard with your name, address, phone number, and the hours you are generally home and the word "HELP" and we will respond as soon as possible. Just write:

Eileen Hershberger
11605 Gowrie Court
Potomac, MD 20854

There is a charge for this personal college counseling service.

Order These Huntington House Books !

——— America Betrayed—Marlin Maddoux	$6.99	———
———• Blessings of Liberty—Charles C. Heath (Paper/Hard cover)	8.99/18.95	———
——— Cover of Darkness (A Novel)—J. Carroll	7.99	———
———• Crystalline Connection (A Novel)—Bob Maddux	8.99	———
——— Deadly Deception: Freemasonry—Tom McKenney	7.99	———
——— The Delicate Balance—John Zajac	8.99	———
——— The Devil's Web—Pat Pulling/Kathy Cawthon	8.99	———
——— Dinosaurs and the Bible—Dave Unfred	12.99	———
———• En Route to Global Occupation—GaryKah	8.99	———
——— Exposing the AIDS Scandal—Dr. Paul Cameron	7.99	———
———• Face the Wind—Gloria Delaney	8.99	———
——— From Rock to Rock—Eric Barger	8.99	———
——— God's Rebels—Henry Lee Curry III, Ph.D.(Paper/		
Hard cover)	12.99/21.99	———
——— Hidden Dangers of the Rainbow—Constance Cumbey	8.99	———
——— The Image of the Ages—David Webber	7.99	———
——— Inside the New Age Nightmare—Randall Baer	8.99	———
———• Journey Into Darkness—Stephen Arrington	8.99	———
——— Jubilee on Wall Street—David Knox Barker	7.99	———
——— Kinsey, Sex and Fraud—Dr. Judith A. Reisman &		
Edward Eichel (Hard cover)	19.99	———
——— Last Days Collection—Last Days Ministries	8.95	———
———• Legend of the Holy Lance (A Novel)—William T. Still		
(Paper/Hard cover)	8.99/16.99	———
——— Lord! Why is My Child a Rebel?	8.99	———
——— New World Order—William T. Still	7.99	———
———• One Year to a College Degree—Lynette Long & Eileen		
Hershberger	8.99	———
——— Personalities in Power—Florence Littauer	8.99	———
———• Political Correctness—David Thibodaux (Paper/Hard cover)	8.99/18.99	———
——— Psychic Phenomena Unveiled—John Anderson	8.99	———
——— Seduction of the Innocent Revisited—John Fulce	8.99	———
———• "Soft Porn" Plays Hardball—Dr. Judith A. Reisman	8.99/16.99	———
(Paper/Hard cover)		
———• Teens and Devil-Worship—Charles G.B. Evans		———
——— To Grow By Storybook Readers—Janet Friend	44.95 per set	———
———• Touching the Face of God—Bob Russell (Paper/	8.99/18.99	———
Hard cover)		
——— Twisted Cross—Joseph Carr	8.99	———
——— Who Will Rule the Future?—Paul McGuire	8.99	———
• New Titles	Shipping and Handling	———
	TOTAL	———

AVAILABLE AT BOOKSTORES EVERYWHERE or order direct from:
Huntington House Publishers • P.O. Box 53788 • Lafayette, LA 70505
Send check/money order. For faster service use VISA/MASTERCARD, call toll-free 1-800-749-4009.

Add: Freight and handling, $3.00 for the first book ordered, and $.50 for each additional book up to 5 books.

Enclosed is $ ————— including postage.

VISA/MASTERCARD# ——————————————————— Exp. Date ——

Name ————————————————————————————————

Address ——————————————————————————————

City, State, Zip code ————————————————————————